Create with Crochet

AMIGURUMI SOFT TOYS

Create with Crochet

AMIGURUMI SOFT TOYS

Landauer Publishing

Articles in this issue are translated or reproduced from *Create with Crochet: Soft Toys Seventh Edition* and are the copyright of or licensed to Future Publishing Limited, a Future plc group company, UK 2023.

Used under license. All rights reserved. This version published by Fox Chapel Publishing Company, Inc., 903 Square Street, Mount Joy, PA 17552.

For more information about the Future plc group, go to **http://www.futureplc.com**.

ISBN 978-1-63981-074-1
Library of Congress Control Number: 2024937752

To learn more about the other great books from Fox Chapel Publishing, or to find a retailer near you, call toll-free 800-457-9112 or visit us at *www.FoxChapelPublishing.com*.

We are always looking for talented authors. To submit an idea, please send a brief inquiry to acquisitions@foxchapelpublishing.com.

Printed in China
First printing

• • INTRODUCTION • •

Amigurumi is the Japanese art of crocheting small, stuffed creatures made of yarn. Literally speaking, *ami* means "knitted" or "crocheted" and *nuigurumi* means "stuffed doll." It has become vastly popular over the last decade, with people able to sell finished products for over $100! More often than not, you will come across adorable translations of your favorite characters, or cartoon versions of real-life animals that make them even cuter than you could possibly imagine. Then, of course, there's the other end of the spectrum, with people taking inanimate objects and giving them the same treatment. Really, the possibilities are endless, and it's super simple, worked mostly in single crochets in the round. With over 30 projects to choose from, there's enough in this book to keep you busy for a long time. So pick up your hook, select your yarn, and get crocheting!

Contents

Getting Started

Throughout this book, all crochet patterns and tutorials use US rather than UK terminology. For notes on converting between US and UK terms, see page 15. There's also a handy list of common abbreviations on page 156 for your guidance.

Pattern Gallery

These star ratings indicate difficulty level, so pick a pattern based on your ability:

Reference

Getting Started

Get a grip on the basics

A crochet hook can feel a bit unnatural in your hand at first, but you'll soon get used to the way it feels.

Yarns

From bulky wool to fingering-weight acrylic, there is a wide variety of yarns with which you can crochet.

To begin crocheting, all you need are two essential pieces of equipment: a crochet hook and a ball of yarn. The yarn that you decide to use will play a part in determining which hook you will work with, so let's start by looking at the many types of yarn available to you.

Yarns are made with a wide variety of fibers; most are natural, some are synthetic, and others blend different fibers together. All yarns have different textures and properties, and will affect the look and feel of your finished project. For example, wool is stretchy and tough, alpaca is soft and luxurious, while natural and synthetic blends are durable with other enhanced properties.

When choosing a yarn, you also need to consider its thickness, usually called its weight. Different weights affect the appearance of your project and the number of stitches needed.

When learning to crochet, it's a good idea to start with a medium-weight yarn that feels comfortable in your hand and is smooth but not too slippery. A yarn described as worsted, Aran, or 10-ply in wool or a wool blend is ideal.

Wool
Wool is very warm and tough, which makes it great for winter wear. It can be fine and soft or rough and scratchy, but will soften with washing. It's mostly affordable, durable, and a good choice for the new crocheter.

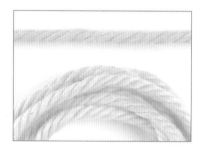

Cotton
This natural vegetable fiber is typically less elastic than wool, and is known for its robustness and washability. Cotton has a lovely stitch definition when crocheted, and is good for homewares and bags. However, it can be a bit hard on the hands.

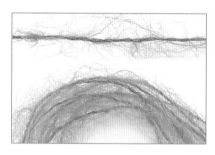

Mohair
Mohair is a silk-like fiber that comes from the Angora goat. It's a yarn that dyes particularly well and is commonly blended with other fibers. It makes for fantastic winter garments, as it is warm and durable.

Acrylic
Made from polyacrylonitrile, acrylic yarn is both affordable and washable. This synthetic yarn is very soft to the touch and comes in a wide variety of colors and textures. Acrylic is commonly blended with other yarns to add durability.

Alpaca
With long and fine fibers, alpaca yarn can sometimes be hairy looking, but it is one of the warmest and most luxurious wools out there. It is also incredibly soft and comes in varieties, such as baby and royal, which are even softer.

Natural and synthetic blends
Blending natural and man-made fibers often creates yarns that are stronger and more versatile. It can also enhance their appearance, making them shinier or more vibrant. Blended yarns are often washable, making them great for garments for children.

Did you know?

Every ball of yarn comes with a recommended hook size, which is printed on the label. It is suggested for amigurumi that you should use a smaller hook to keep the gauge tight so you can't see the stuffing.

Yarn weights

Yarn weight	Properties	Ideal for	Recommended hook sizes US	UK
Lace, fingering, 1-ply to 3-ply	Extremely light, lace yarn produces a very delicate texture on a US 0 (2mm) hook. A bigger hook will produce a more open fabric.	Lace	B/1	2.25mm
Super fine, sock, fingering, baby, 4-ply	Using very slim needles, super fine yarn is perfect for lightweight, intricate lace work.	Finely woven socks, shawls, babywear	B/1 to E/4	2.25–3.5mm
Fine, sport, baby, 5-ply	Fine yarn is great for socks, and can also be used in items that feature slightly more delicate textures.	Light jumpers, babywear, socks, accessories	E/4 to 7	3.5–4.5mm
Light, double knit (DK), light worsted, 8-ply	An extremely versatile weight of yarn, DK can be used to create a wide variety of items and crochets relatively quickly.	Sweaters, lightweight scarves, blankets, toys	7 to I/9	4.5–5.5mm
Medium, worsted, Aran, Afghan, 10-ply to12-ply	With many yarns in this thickness using a variety of fibers to make them machine washable, worsted yarn is good for garments with thick cabled detail and for functional items.	Sweaters, cabled garments, blankets, hats, scarves, mittens	I-9 to K/10 ½	5.5–6.5mm
Bulky, chunky, craft, rug, 12-ply to 14-ply	Quick to crochet, bulky yarn is perfect for warm outerwear. Often made from lightweight fibers to prevent drooping.	Rugs, jackets, blankets, hats, leg warmers, winter accessories	K/10 ½ to M/13	6.5–9mm
Super bulky, super chunky, roving, 14-ply to 16-ply	Commonly used with very large hooks, super bulky yarn crochets very quickly. Large stitches make mistakes easy to spot.	Heavy blankets, rugs, thick scarves	M/13+	9mm+

Amigurumi kit bag

Although just a hook and a ball of yarn will get you pretty far in crochet, many other helpful tools are available.

Case

You will only need a small case to keep all your crochet tools together, and ones designed with crochet tools in mind can be found at most craft stores. These will most likely be fitted with multiple elastic straps to keep your hooks and tools in place. However, as crochet hooks are small, you could use a pencil case (as pictured below) to keep everything in one place.

Row counter

Row counters are used for marking how many rows you've worked. Just turn it once when you finish a row and it will keep track for you.

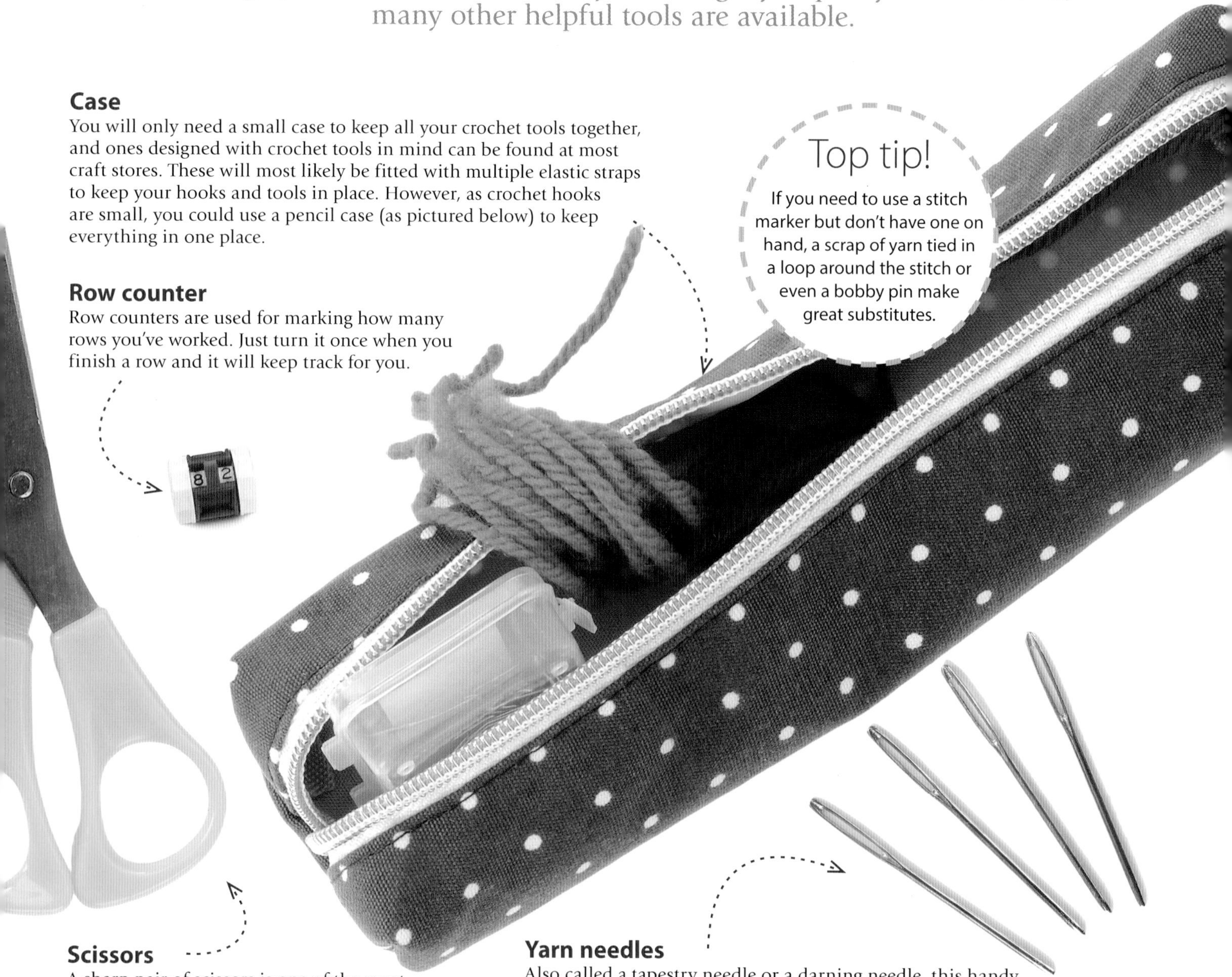

Top tip!

If you need to use a stitch marker but don't have one on hand, a scrap of yarn tied in a loop around the stitch or even a bobby pin make great substitutes.

Scissors

A sharp pair of scissors is one of the most important tools a crocheter can keep on hand, as you will use them frequently for cutting yarn. Try to avoid using a blunt pair, as this can cause yarn to fray, making it difficult to work with.

Yarn needles

Also called a tapestry needle or a darning needle, this handy tool will be useful for finishing off your projects neatly. As these needles are thick, blunt-tipped, and have a large eye to fit the yarn into, they are the perfect tool for weaving in ends and stitching pieces together, giving a professional finish to your pieces.

Stitch markers

With multiple uses, stitch markers are some of the handiest tools a crocheter can keep in their kit bag. Their main purpose is to mark stitches. Place one in the first stitch of a row so you don't lose your place in a pattern.

Fiberfill

For stuffing your amigurumi projects, you will need toy stuffing, also known as fiberfill. You can buy it in craft stores or simply use the stuffing from a pillow!

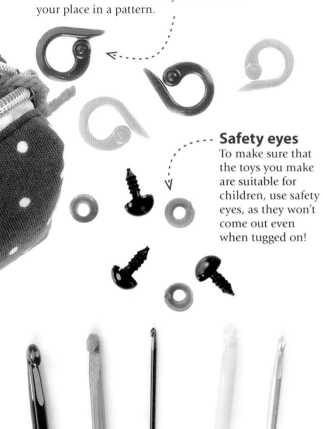

Safety eyes

To make sure that the toys you make are suitable for children, use safety eyes, as they won't come out even when tugged on!

Hook sizes

Hook sizes are measured by the width across the shank. In the US, hooks are listed with letter and number sizes that correspond to the mm measurements used for UK hooks. The smallest sizes measure around 2mm, while the largest sizes measure over 20mm. The table below shows how the US and UK sizes compare. The size of hook you will need is related to the thickness of yarn that you use—thicker yarns need larger hooks. It is suggested that you use a smaller hook than recommended for amigurumi projects—the patterns will tell you what this smaller hook size is for each project.

Hook size table:

US size	UK size
B/1	2mm, 2.25mm
C/2	2.5mm, 2.75mm
D/3	3mm, 3.25mm
E/4	3.5mm
F/5	3.75mm, 4mm
G/6	4mm, 4.25mm
G/7	4.5mm
H/8	5mm
I/9	5.5mm
J/10	6mm
K/10 ½	6.5mm, 7mm
L/11	8mm
M/13	9mm
N,P/15	10mm

Hook materials

As well as varying in size and style, crochet hooks also come in a variety of materials, most commonly metal, plastic, and wood—each with their own set of pros and cons. You can also get hooks that come with a rubber handle, which provide a more comfortable grip for larger projects. To determine which type of hook is best for you, give each a try to see which feels the most comfortable in your hand before you invest in multiple sizes.

How to read a pattern

Most crochet projects are made by following a pattern. Although they may look daunting at first, they're easy to read once you understand the terms.

When you've decided on what you want your first crochet project to be—whether it's a simple scarf or an amigurumi character—you will most likely follow a pattern to create it. Patterns are the instructions that tell you what stitches to use and how to combine them to make the item you're working on. You can find amigurumi patterns starting on page 54 in this book.

As crochet patterns are written in shorthand, to the untrained eye they can just look like meaningless lists of jumbled letters, but they're actually pretty accessible once you've mastered the terms. They are written this way so they won't take up too much space on the page, and also to make them easier to follow. Instead of a long list of words that you could easily lose your place in, patterns are concise and simple to read. All patterns should follow the same conventions, so once you've learned how to read them, any that you pick up should make sense. Read on to learn all about crochet patterns.

Starting instructions

At the top of a stitch pattern will normally be very important information that you need to know before beginning work on the pattern. This will include what size hook and weight of yarn is recommended, as well as the gauge. There may also be information about any special stitches you need and any uncommon abbreviations.

To begin your pattern, the first instruction will usually be to create a foundation chain (for working in rows) or a chain circle or magic ring (for working in the round). If you are not working to exact measurements laid out in the pattern, you will be told to make a foundation chain in a multiple. This is needed to ensure that any repeats don't get cut off halfway through when you come to the end of a row, as well as a small number of stitches for the turning chain. For example, "ch a multiple of 6 sts plus 3" means you need to chain any multiple of six (6, 12, 18, 24, etc.), plus three more chains at the end for the turning chain.

Rows and rounds

Crochet is always worked either in rows or rounds, and patterns give you the instructions for what you should do in each row or round you are about to create. They will be numbered (Row 1, Row 2 or Rnd 1, Rnd 2, etc.) to make it easy for you to keep your place when working through the list. At the end of each instruction, the number of stitches you should have worked in that round/row will be given. If you have crocheted more or fewer than this, then you know a mistake has been made. This gives you an opportunity to correct it before you move on.

Working into specific stitches

As well as telling you which stitch to make next, a pattern will also tell you where to make it.

If the pattern says to work into the next stitch, you need to crochet into the very next stitch. For example, "dc in next st" means double crochet in the next stitch.

If it says to work a multiple of stitches into a multiple number of stitches, you need to crochet the same stitch however many times it asks for into the number of stitches it asks you to. For example, "2 tr in next 2 sts" means make two treble crochets in the next stitch and two treble crochets in the one after it, for a total of four stitches made.

When different stitch types are given in parentheses, you need to make all of the stitches given in the stitch it's asking you to. For example, "(tr, ch, tr) in next st" means make a treble crochet in the next stitch, then chain, then treble crochet in the same stitch as the first treble crochet.

If a pattern asks you to work a stitch into a specific stitch, then you skip all the ones that come before and work it into the top of the stitch it's asking you to. For example, 'dc in next tr' means double crochet in the next treble crochet, no matter what comes before it in the row.

If a pattern asks you to work the next stitch into a chain space (ch-sp), then you need to insert your hook in the space underneath a loop that was created by a chain in the row below.

Repeats

Instead of writing out repeated instructions, they will be identified in patterns either using parentheses or an asterisk (or other symbol), followed by an instruction of how many times they should be repeated within your chosen pattern.

Repeated instructions given in parentheses—for example, "(2 dc in next st, tr in next st) 4 times"—means that the sequence inside the parentheses needs to be followed, from beginning to end, as many times as identified by the number outside the parentheses. In this case, four times.

Repeated instructions identified with an asterisk—for example, "*tr in next 4 chs, ch 2, sk next 2 chs; rep from * 3 times"—means that the sequence that begins at the asterisk and ends at the semicolon needs to be followed, and then repeated the number of times stated. So in this case, the instruction will be followed four times.

Repeated instructions can also direct that they be worked until the end of the row, or until the last few stitches. For example, "*3tr in next st, ch 2, dc in next st; rep from * across to

There is no stitch called a single crochet (sc) in UK terminology.

last 2 sts, tr in last 2 sts" means you repeat the sequence between the asterisk and semicolon until you reach the last two stitches of the row (or round), at which point you end the repeat and follow the further instructions.

Multiple sizes

A pattern may offer you multiple sizes to make something in, which is particularly common with items for infants and young children. When this happens, the information for the smallest size will be given first with the rest following in parentheses. For example, "Size: Small (medium, large) ch 40 (48, 56)."

This means that to make the smallest item, you need to follow the first instruction, for the medium size, the first instruction inside the parentheses, and for the largest, the second instruction given inside the parentheses. Make sure to not use the wrong instruction, or else you may find the garment won't fit.

US/UK terminology
Follow the pattern

Confusingly, patterns that are printed in Britain and other places that follow UK naming conventions use different terms to describe stitches than patterns printed in North America. To make things even more difficult, the same name is used to mean different stitches under either convention. Most patterns will state whether they are using US or UK terminology at the start, but if not, checking the pattern's country of origin may be a good place to start in finding out which convention is being used. A handy trick to remember is that there is no stitch called a single crochet (sc) in UK terminology, so if you see this on the pattern, then you know it is using US naming conventions. **NOTE:** Everything in this book uses US terminology.

Always make sure you check whether a crochet pattern uses US or UK crochet terms—or you'll find yourself very confused.

US	UK
Chain (ch)	Chain (ch)
Single crochet (sc)	Double crochet (dc)
Half double crochet (hdc)	Half treble crochet (hdc)
Double crochet (dc)	Treble crochet (tr)
Treble (or triple) crochet (tr)	Double treble crochet (dtr)
Slip stitch (ss or sl st)	Slip stitch (ss or sl st)

Foundation chain

When working in rows or starting certain patterns in the round, you will need to create a foundation chain to work your first row of stitches into.

Make a chain Start your very first stitch

01 Start with a slipknot
The first step is to create a slipknot on your hook.

02 Yarn over
Move your hook underneath your yarn to create a yarn over.

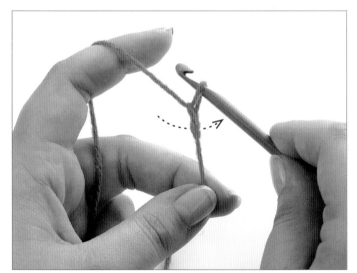

03 Pull through
Move the hook back through the loop already on your hook, making sure to catch the working yarn. You have now made your first chain.

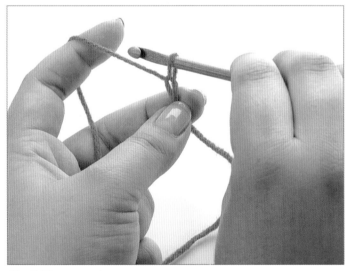

04 Keep going
Repeat Steps 2 and 3 to make more chains. Hold the stitches you've already made in your left hand close to the hook for stability. Your pattern will tell you how many you need to chain.

Make the chain correctly Don't let it get tangled

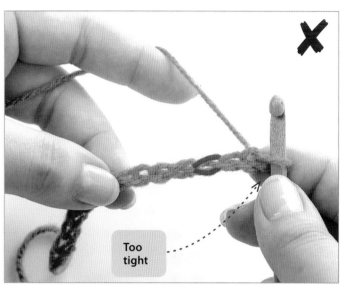

Too tight

01 Even stitches
Try to make all the chains a similar size to ensure you are making a strong foundation for your piece. If some are very loose and others aren't, the effect will be a wavy edge to your piece. This will take some practice.

The wrong way
It's best to keep the chains quite loose to begin with, as tight chains will be very difficult to make stitches into when it comes to the next row, as you will struggle to insert your hook into them and pull it through again.

Counting chains

When beginning a project, the pattern you are following will tell you how many chains you need to create, either in total or as a multiple. It's important to create exactly the right number, as getting this wrong will mean you have to unravel your work when you find out you've either got too many or not enough at the end of your first row. To count the chains, identify the Vs on the side that's facing you. Each of these is one chain. The V above the slipknot is your first chain, but do not count the loop on your hook. This is the working loop and does not count as a chain. If you are creating a very long chain, it might help to mark every ten or 20 stitches with a stitch marker.

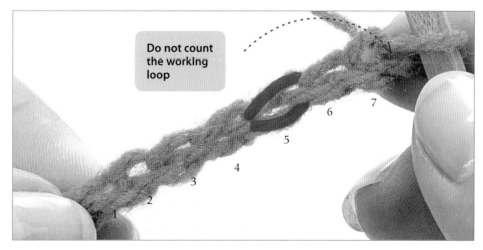

Do not count the working loop

Turning chain height

Different stitches need different heights of turning chains, which accommodates for the height of the stitch about to be made itself. However, the standard turning chain heights may not always work for you, as it depends on how loosely or tightly you create chain stitches. If you find your turning chains bulge out of the fabric, try chaining one less than specified. Alternatively, if they are tight and distorting the edge of the fabric, try chaining one more than specified. Use the table to find the standard turning chain lengths for basic stitches.

Stitch (US)	Number of turning chains
Single crochet (sc)	1
Half double crochet (hdc)	2
Double crochet (dc)	3
Treble crochet (tr)	4

Getting Started

Chain anatomy Get to know the parts of the chain

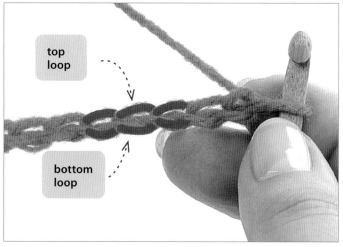

01 Front of the chain
Looking at the front side of your chain, you will see a row of sideways Vs, each with a top loop and a bottom loop.

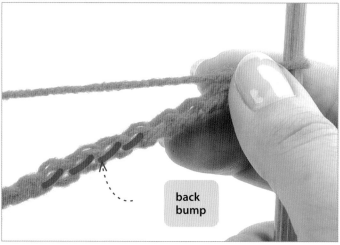

02 Back of the chain
When you look at the back side of the chain, you will see a line of bumps in between the loops. These are called the back bumps.

Under the top loop Use the most common way to work the chain

01 Find the top loop
For this method, hook under the top loop only.

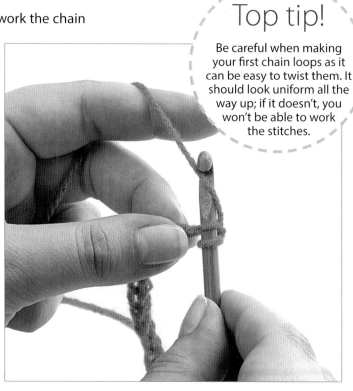

02 Insert your hook
Move your hook to insert it under the top loop of a V.

Top tip!
Be careful when making your first chain loops as it can be easy to twist them. It should look uniform all the way up; if it doesn't, you won't be able to work the stitches.

Under the top loop and back bump Work the chain differently

Top tip!

Working under the top loop is the easiest method for beginners, but does not create as neat an edge as working under the back bumps.

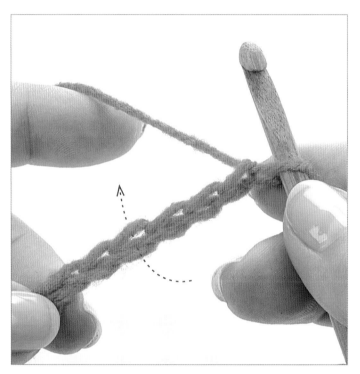

01 Under two
Hooking under both the top loop and the back bump is sometimes referred to as the top two loops of the chain.

02 Insert your hook
Move your hook to insert it under the back bump and top loop of a chain.

Under the back bump Work the chain in reverse

01 Find the back bump
Turn over your chain so that the back bumps are facing you.

02 Insert your hook
Move your hook to insert it under the back bump.

Working into subsequent rows

When you've completed your first row, the only way is up. The next step is to build on the row you've just worked.

To work into the row you've just crocheted, you will first need to crochet a turning chain (t-ch), which you can learn how to create on page 17. When you've made this the length suggested on the pattern for the stitch that you are working, you will then crochet into the row you just created in a very similar way to working into the foundation chain.

When looking at the top of the row, you will see the Vs of the stitches. To work into the next row, you can either crochet under the back loop, under the front loop, or under both loops of the stitch on the row below. If your pattern doesn't specify which loops to work into, the standard way is to insert your hook under both, as crocheting under one creates a ridge along the base of the row from the unworked loops.

Top tip!

There can be several V shapes when looking at your yarn. To identify your stitch, look at the hook and where the threads meet from that loop—work into that V.

Under the front and back loops

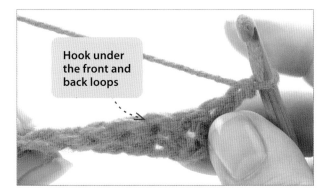

Hook under the front and back loops

01 Under both
Hooking under the front and back loops of the stitch is the most common way to work into a row.

02 Insert your hook
After the turning chain (as illustrated in Step 1), insert your hook so that it goes in under both the front and back loops of the V.

Under the front loops only (flo)

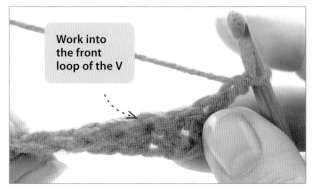

Work into the front loop of the V

01 Identify the front loop
Working into the front loop of the V only creates a ridge along the bottom of the row on the side of the work that is facing away from you.

02 Insert your hook
Make sure your hook only goes under the front loop of the V.

Under the back loops only (blo)

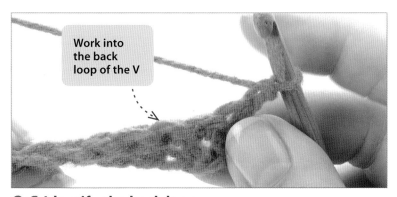

Work into the back loop of the V

01 Identify the back loop
Working into the back loop of the V only creates a ridge along the bottom of the row on the side of the work that's facing you.

02 Insert your hook
Make sure your hook only goes under the back loop on the V.

Yarn over

This is the single most basic step in creating crochet stitches, and a technique that's important to master before moving on.

Make a yarn over Master the essential crochet technique

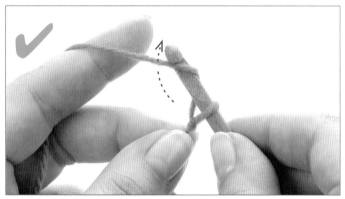

01 Move your hook, not the yarn
While it sounds like a yarn over (yo) should be made by moving the yarn over the hook, it's easier to keep the yarn still and guide the crochet hook around it. With your hook in your right hand and the working yarn in your left, pass your hook underneath the yarn from right to left.

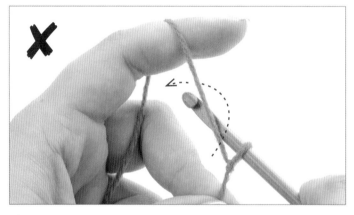

The wrong way
Moving the hook under the yarn from left to right will make creating stitches incredibly difficult, and if you do manage it, then the stitches that you have created will become twisted and tangled.

02 Make another
There will be times when you need to yarn over twice, and to do this, just repeat the motion from Step 1, making sure to move the hook from right to left.

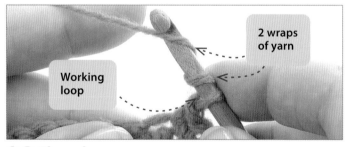

2 wraps of yarn

Working loop

03 Three loops
After two yarn overs, there will be three loops on your hook: the working loop and the two that you just made by wrapping the yarn over twice.

04 Drawing up a loop
To draw up a loop, you need to insert your hook into the stitch indicated on your pattern, create a yarn over, and then move your hook back through the work, making sure to catch the yarn over in the throat of your hook. There will now be two loops on your hook—the loop that you have just drawn up and the one you started with.

Slip stitch

While rarely used on its own to create a pattern, this versatile stitch is really handy for joining stitches and moving the position of the hook and yarn without adding height.

Make a slip stitch Work a stitch made for construction not height

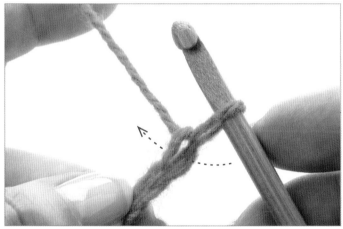

01 Foundation chain
Make a foundation chain to the required length. For a precise number of stitches, chain that many plus one. Identify the second chain from your hook.

02 Into chain
Insert your hook into the second chain from the hook. Yarn over (yo).

03 Draw up a loop
Pull your hook back through the chain. There should be two loops on your hook.

04 Pull through
Avoiding the urge to yarn over, continue to pull the yarn through the second loop on the hook. You have completed the stitch and should have one loop on your hook.

Single crochet

The easiest crochet stitch creates short and compact stitches.

Single crochet (sc) is a very important stitch in crochet as it is one of the simplest, and therefore the one that most crocheters tend to learn to use first. Mastering this stitch will also help you when it comes to creating taller stitches, as most are created by just adding steps to the method for making a single crochet. Using only single crochets creates a very compact, dense fabric, which makes it great for thick, warm winter garments. It is also the most common stitch in amigurumi and toy making, as the compact fabric created is very good for holding stuffing in.

For these types of projects, be sure to use a smaller hook than recommended by the yarn manufacturer (see page 43).

If you plan to single crochet into a foundation chain, as we will in this tutorial, then you will need to make one more chain than the number of stitches you want to create, as the first stitch is never worked into the first chain from the hook. However, this will be accounted for in a pattern, so always chain the number stated.

Make a single crochet   The essential amigurumi stitch

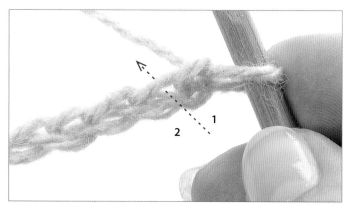

01 Foundation chain
Make a foundation chain to the required length. If you just want to practice, start by making about 20 chains. If you want to make a piece exactly 20 stitches wide, chain 21.

02 Insert hook
Identify the second chain from your hook and then insert your hook here.

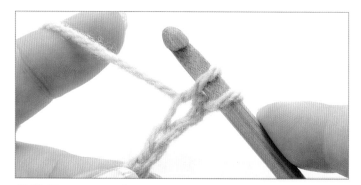

03 Draw up a loop
Yarn over (yo), then draw up a loop. You will now have two loops on your crochet hook.

04 Pull through two
Yarn over and then draw the yarn through both loops on the hook so you have one loop left on your hook. You have completed the stitch.

Top tip!

For your single crochet turning chain, you only need to complete one stitch to take the row up before working your next single crochets.

Turning chain

06 Time to turn
Turn your work counterclockwise, so that the next stitches ready to be worked into are to the left of the hook.

05 Keep going
Continue making single crochets by inserting your hook into each remaining chain and repeating Steps 3 and 4. When you have finished the row, chain one.

07 Start a new row
Identify the first stitch of the row (not the turning chain). Insert your hook here.

08 Repeat
Follow Steps 3 and 4 to complete the stitch.

Double crochet

This stitch is twice the size of the single crochet, and worked in a very similar way.

The double crochet (dc) is a very common stitch that is simple to create, especially once you've mastered the technique of making a single crochet (sc). It is created simply by adding a couple of steps to the method for creating a single crochet.

Due to its increased height, this stitch creates a much less compact and therefore more versatile fabric than the single crochet. It is a very common and recognizable stitch, as seen

in granny squares. When working a double crochet into a foundation chain, you must make two more chains than your desired number of stitches. This is because a double crochet is usually worked into the fourth chain from the hook when being worked into a foundation chain, and the three unworked chains will form your first double crochet stitch.

Make a double crochet Building up your skill

01 Foundation chain
Make a foundation chain to the required length. For a precise number of stitches, chain that many plus two. Find the fourth chain from the hook.

02 Yarn over
Make a yarn over (yo), and then insert your hook into the fourth chain from the hook.

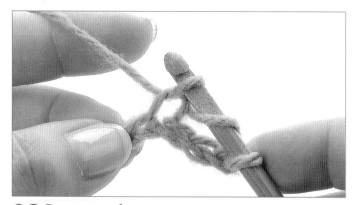

03 Draw up a loop
Yarn over, then draw up a loop. There should now be three loops on your hook.

04 Pull through two
Yarn over, then draw the yarn through two of the loops on your hook. There should now be two loops on your hook.

This stitch creates a much less compact and therefore more versatile fabric than the single crochet.

05 Complete the stitch

Yarn over and then draw the yarn through the two loops left on the hook. You have completed the stitch and should now have one loop on your hook.

06 Keep going

Continue making double crochets by making a yarn over and then inserting your hook into each remaining chain and repeating Steps 3 to 5. When you have finished the row, chain three.

07 Turn

Turn your work counterclockwise so you are ready to start the next row. The two chains you just made count as the first stitch, so your next stitch will need to be made in the second stitch of the row.

08 Continue down the row

Yarn over, put your hook into the next stitch, and repeat Steps 3 to 5 to make the stitch. Continue to the end of the row, remembering to put the final double crochet into the top of the turning chain of the row below.

Half double crochet

A less common stitch that is taller than single crochet
but not quite as tall as double crochet.

This stitch is strange when compared to the single crochet (sc) and double crochet (dc) in the way that it's made. Instead of drawing a loop through two loops, the yarn is instead pulled through three to create a half double crochet (hdc). This produces a stitch that's about half as tall as the double crochet, but taller than the single crochet. This can be quite tricky to get the hang of the first time, so a little practice may be necessary. When used on its own, the half double crochet produces a fairly compact fabric, which is similar in texture to that created when

using single crochet by itself. Mastering the techniques used to create the single and double crochet will help greatly when creating the half double crochet.

Like with working a single crochet into a foundation chain, you will need to make one more chain than your desired number of stitches. This is because the double crochet will be worked into the third chain from the hook, and the two unworked chains will form your first half double crochet stitch.

Make a half double crochet Combining techniques

01 Foundation chain
Make a foundation chain to the required length, not forgetting to chain one more than the number of stitches you desire. Identify the third chain from the hook.

02 Yarn over
Make a yarn over (yo), and then insert your hook into the third chain from the hook.

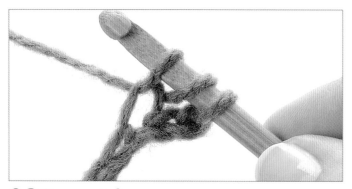

03 Draw up a loop
Yarn over, then draw up a loop. There should now be three loops on your hook.

04 Pull through three
Yarn over, then draw the yarn through all three loops on your hook. The stitch is now complete, and there should be one loop on your hook.

05 Keep going
Continue making half double crochets by making a yarn over, inserting your hook into each remaining chain and repeating Steps 3 and 4. When you have finished the row, chain two.

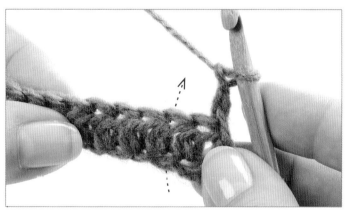

06 Turn
Turn your work counterclockwise so you are ready to start the next row. The two chains you just made count as the first stitch, so your next stitch will need to be made in the second stitch of the row.

07 Start new row
Yarn over and insert your hook into the second stitch of the row.

Top tip!
When working with hdc in the round, you will want to use multiples of eight stitches for it to lay flat.

08 Continue to crochet
Repeat Steps 3 and 4 to complete the stitch.

Treble (or triple) crochet

This common stitch is much taller than the double crochet, and this size allows it to be worked into a piece of fabric fairly quickly.

While the other stitches you have learned create quite close, compact stitches, the treble crochet (tr) creates very tall stitches that make a loose, stretchy fabric. For this reason, the treble crochet is most often found in lace work.

The treble crochet is created by making two yarn overs (yo) before inserting the hook into the stitch or chain below, and this can make it quite difficult to work with. It's important to check that you have the correct number of loops on your hook after you've drawn up the first loop, as it's very easy for the second yarn over to slip off the hook before you insert it

into your fabric, without you even noticing. However, this is a valuable stitch because when compared to the single crochet (sc), which works up rather slowly, it's very easy to create a large piece of fabric quickly with the treble crochet.

When creating a foundation chain to work treble crochets into, you need to make three more chains than the desired number of stitches, as the first stitch will be worked into the fifth chain from the hook, with the four chains making the first treble crochet.

Make a treble crochet Master the longest crochet stitch

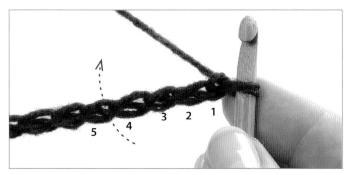

01 Foundation chain
Make a foundation chain to the required length, making sure to chain three more than the number of stitches you need. Identify the fifth chain from the hook.

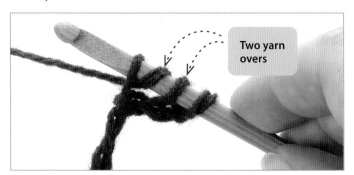

02 Yarn over twice
Make two yarn overs and then insert your hook into the fifth chain from the hook.

03 Draw up a loop
Yarn over and draw up a loop. There should be four loops on your hook.

04 Pull through two

Yarn over, then draw the yarn through two of the loops on your hook. There should now be three loops on your hook.

05 And again ...

Yarn over, then draw the yarn through two of the loops on your hook again. There should now be two loops on your hook.

06 ... and once more

Yarn over, then draw the yarn through the two loops on your hook. There should now be one loop on your hook.

07 Complete the row

Repeat Steps 2 through 6 into each remaining chain to finish the row. When you reach the end of the row, chain four and turn your work clockwise. The chain four counts as the first stitch, so you will need to make the next into the second stitch from the end.

08 Carry on crocheting

Yarn over twice, insert the hook into the second stitch from the end of the row, and repeat Steps 3 through 6 to complete the stitch.

Starting in the round

There are two options when working in the round, both of which you can apply to all of your amigurumi projects.

When you are working in the round, you have two options for how to start your project. Usually a pattern will tell you which it would prefer for you to begin with—a chain or a magic ring, both of which will be covered on the following pages.

The most simple method to begin with is a chain, which will see you connect a short chain together into a circle and work your first round into the middle of the chain. The second method, starting with a magic ring, is a little more complicated, but it produces a tighter first round and a more secure final product. It sees you work your stitches onto a loop of yarn, which you later pull tight before proceeding to work your stitches into the round.

It should be pointed out that if you find that you prefer one method over the other, and a project suggests you use the one you aren't so keen on, it wouldn't actually affect the final product too much to use the alternate method. Do what feels most comfortable.

Single chain start Begin your circular project with a single chain

Work all the stitches into this chain

01 Make a chain
Chain two.

02 Double crochet
Now make a single crochet (sc) into the second chain from your hook.

Top tip!
Do not work into the individual chains when starting your project with a multiple chain start. This will create a rather ugly extra first round that you don't want.

03 Continue into the chain
Make the rest of your single crochets into the same chain stitch as your first single crochet.

Multiple chain start Create a ring using multiple chains

01 Create a chain
Make a short chain, depending on the pattern that you're following. Here we have shown five chains.

02 Slip stitch
Create a slip stitch (sl st) into the first chain that you created.

03 Into the center
Work your first round into the middle of the ring you have created. Now either continue to work in a spiral, or connect the last single crochet to the first with a slip stitch, create your turning chains, and continue on.

Did you know?

Crochet isn't just fun, it's good for you, too! It has been proven to help with your hand-eye coordination and even your math skills.

Getting Started

Magic ring Start your project with a bit of "magic"

01 Make a loop
To begin, create a loop (as if to create a slipknot), hold the yarn where the loop crosses over, with the starting tail in front, and then insert your needle from front to back.

02 Yarn over
With the working yarn, yarn over (yo) your hook and pull up a loop back through to the front. Make sure you are not using the starting yarn—this will simply unravel.

03 Make your first stitch
Yarn over your hook again, this time from above the loop, and pull through to create a chain on your ring.

Use longer stitches
When starting with a magic ring, you can create more chains in Step 3 and continue to use the extra length to use longer stitches in your project. For instance, if you want to use half double crochets (hdc), you can chain 2; chain 3 for a double crochet (dc) and chain 4 for a treble (tr).

04 Insert your hook
To create your first single crochet (sc), insert your hook into the ring, with both the loop and starting tail above your hook. Your stitches will now be created around both yarns.

05 Crochet a stitch
Yarn over and draw up a loop back to the front of the ring. Create your stitch as you would usually.

06 Keep going
Carry on with the previous two steps until you have created your ring.

07 Secure
Once you have created all of your stitches, keep your hook in the loop and hold it and your round in your dominant hand. Now pull on the starting tail until the gap is closed. Continue working as shown on page 40.

Increasing

To increase the number of stitches in a row, simply crochet two or more stitches into the same stitch.

Increasing is a very useful technique in crochet and one that's incredibly easy to execute. Increasing is essential when working in the round to create something flat, as the extra stitches add width. Without increasing, you would just build upward, not outward. Increasing is also very useful when shaping items—such as amigurumi—as it can be combined with decreases to make the shapes you need.

To increase the number of stitches in your round or row, simply crochet two or more stitches into one stitch of the row below. For example, if you have just crocheted a round of eight stitches, then crochet two of each stitch into each stitch below—your next round will have 16 stitches. In patterns, increasing is written as the number of stitches to be made into the stitch below. For example, "2tr in next st."

Standard Increases Keep in the round work flat

When you're working in the round, you will need to make sure that you add a certain number of stitches to each round in order to keep your work flat (if this is the desired effect). Adding too many stitches will result in your work starting to ruffle, but not adding enough will result in a ball starting to form, which is actually perfect for amigurumi, so make sure you check the pattern if you think you have taken a wrong turn.

The number of stitches that you add per row depends on what type of stitch you have used. Refer to the table (at right) to decipher how many stitches you will need to add each round.

Stitch	Stitches in first round	Increases in subsequent rounds
Single	6	6
Half double	8	8
Double	12	12
Treble	18	18

Top tip!

Making lots of increases in one place will make bulges (and shells), so if you just want to make the piece larger without distorting the fabric, spread your increases out across the length of the round or row.

Adding stitches Make a double crochet increase in the next stitch (2 dc in next st)

01 **Double crochet**
Make a double crochet in the next stitch.

02 **Into the same stitch**
Make another double crochet in the same stitch. You have increased your stitch count by one.

Increasing at the start of a row Make a double crochet increase in the next stitch (2 dc in next st)

01 **Chain three and turn**
As the turning chain normally counts as a stitch (except in single crochet), increasing at the start of a row is slightly different.

02 **Into the first stitch**
Where you would normally make your first stitch into the second stitch from the hook, to increase, insert your hook into the first stitch at the base of the chain and make the stitch.

03 **Two stitches**
The stitch you've just made and the turning chain count as two stitches, and you have made an increase.

Decreasing

- -

Often worked in conjunction with increases when shaping crochet,
decrease stitches reduce the number of stitches in a row.

While the easiest way to reduce the number of stitches in a row is to simply skip stitches, this creates a hole, which is not always the desired effect. To avoid this hole, decrease stitches work multiple stitches together, thereby eliminating stitches while also filling in the gap. Decrease stitches are named after the number and type of stitches being crocheted together. For example, "sc2tog"

means that two single crochet stitches will be combined into one. When the number in the middle increases, this means even more stitches will be crocheted into one. While decreases have many different names and forms, the basic formula is the same: make all the stitches up to the final step so that they are all on the hook, then complete all the stitches together.

Single crochet two stitches together Combine two single crochet stitches (sc2tog)

01 Insert hook
Insert your hook into the next stitch, as if to make a single crochet. Draw up a loop.

02 Insert hook again
Without completing the stitch, insert your hook into the next stitch as if to make another single crochet. Draw up a loop. You should now have three loops on your hook.

03 Through three
Yarn over (yo) and draw the loop through all three stitches on your hook. Having worked into two stitches, but only created one, you have decreased by one.

Double crochet three stitches together Combine three stitches (dc3tog)

01 Insert hook
Yarn over and insert your hook into the next stitch, as if to make a double crochet. Draw up a loop, yarn over and draw through two loops on the hook. There should now be two loops on your hook.

02 Insert hook again
Without completing the stitch, yarn over and insert your hook into the next stitch. Draw up a loop, yarn over and draw through two loops on the hook. There should now be three loops on your hook.

03 And again
Repeat Step 2 into the next stitch. There should now be four loops on your hook, for three incomplete double crochet stitches.

04 Pull through four
Yarn over and draw the yarn through all four loops on the hook to complete the decrease. Having worked into three stitches, but only created one, you have decreased your stitch count by two.

Working in the round

Following on from your chain start or magic ring, start working in the round.

Amigurumi is the main type of crochet projects that uses working in the round. While most patterns will use a continuous spiral method, some will use joined rounds as well.

Working in a spiral works best when you are working with single crochet (sc) stitches because larger stitches are harder to disguise at the end of the rounds. Having said that, if you have to do it, it isn't impossible (see the example on page 41). At the end of your work, you will hide the last jog of stitches with an invisible finish.

Working in joined rounds works well when you are using longer stitches. It consists of joining the tops of the stitches together at the end of each round, and using a collection of chains in order to create the first stitch of the next round.

When working in the round, to produce flat pieces you will need a certain amount of increases, which you can see on page 36.

Here we will show you both techniques. Your pattern may not specify whether to use a spiral or joined technique, but it will become obvious if you are asked to join each round with a slip stitch.

Continuous spiral Keep your circular projects going in one long "line"

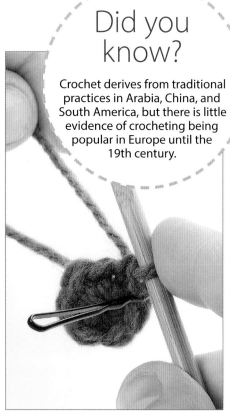

Did you know?

Crochet derives from traditional practices in Arabia, China, and South America, but there is little evidence of crocheting being popular in Europe until the 19th century.

01 Crochet your round
Crochet each of your stitches into your chain start or magic ring. If you're using single crochets, use six stitches, for half doubles (hdc), use eight, and for doubles (dc), use 12.

02 Start the next round
To start each new round, work the first stitch into the top of the first stitch of the last round. Now add your stitch marker into this stitch by slipping it through the stitch as you would crochet into it on the next round.

03 Continue your pattern
Now continue to stitch the rest of your round as stated in the pattern. Here we are doing two single crochets into each stitch.

04 Work the end of the round
Continue around until you reach the stitch before the marker you inserted earlier. This is the last stitch of the round.

05 Start the next round
To stitch your next round, remove the marker, crochet the stitch as normal, and then replace the marker into the stitch you have just created.

06 Finishing your spiral
To finish your spiral, you will need to smooth out the jump in stitches between rows. To do so, slip stitch into the next stitch. For taller stitches, gradually crochet shorter stitches as shown in the two images on the left.

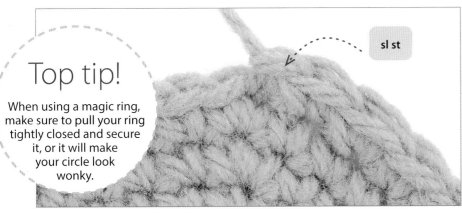

sl st

Top tip!
When using a magic ring, make sure to pull your ring tightly closed and secure it, or it will make your circle look wonky.

Single crochet spiral
To end a single crochet spiral, simply slip stitch into the next stitch to hide the jog between rows.

sl st

sc

hdc

Double crochet spiral
If you have worked your spiral using double crochets, you will need to end your spiral with a half double crochet, single crochet, slip stitch.

Getting Started

Working in joined rounds Use slip stitches to join your rounds

01 Crochet your first round
Finish your first round, stitching double crochets into your rounding ring.

02 Make a slip stitch
To join the rows, make a slip stitch into the top of the first stitch of the round—this will be as if you are creating the next stitch for single crochet—or into the top of the turning chain for any longer stitches.

03 Completed round
Now you have finished your first round and created your circle.

04 Start round two
To create your next round, create a chain to the height of your stitch. One for single, two for half double, three for double, and so on.

Amigurumi gauge

To ensure you get the best results from your amigurumi creations, it's important to understand a little about gauge (tension).

Unlike when making larger crochet projects or garments, achieving exact gauge is not as critical for amigurumi. However, it is important to note that your gauge should always be quite tight, and this is achieved by using a smaller size hook than you might otherwise expect, and smaller than that recommended on the ball band of your yarn. For example, a DK weight yarn might usually be worked on a G/6 (4mm) hook, but for amigurumi, you might use a D/3 (3mm) hook or even smaller.

A tight gauge helps prevent the amigurumi figure from being floppy, which is particularly important for figures that are to sit upright. Too loose a gauge and you will be able to see the stuffing through the small gaps between stitches; your project may turn out considerably larger than anticipated; and you may also use more yarn than the pattern recommends.

The hook size listed in patterns is only a recommendation, or starting point. It is important to remember that everyone has their own stitching tension, leading to different gauges—some people crochet more tightly or loosely than others. This is normal and not a problem, you just need to be aware of it and know how to adjust your gauge to that required. This is easily achieved by using a smaller or larger hook.

Top tip!

Your pattern will advise you what size hook to use, but if varying the yarn weight, go down a size or two from the recommended size on the yarn you use.

Gauge too loose

If you crochet at a normal or loose gauge, you will find that you will be able to see the stuffing between the stitches, which detracts from the finished appearance of your project. If your crochet looks like this, you should consider using a smaller hook than the one suggested by the pattern.

Correct gauge

Here you will see the stitches are much closer together and so the stuffing is barely visible. It's difficult to be too tight with amigurumi, however you should still be able to work stitches reasonably easily. If you are working too tightly, this can feel difficult and uncomfortable on your hands, and you should consider changing to a larger hook.

Fixing mistakes

A benefit of crochet is how easy it is to undo mistakes—all you have to do is unravel to the point where you messed up, then make it right!

One of the joys of crochet patterns is that they are designed to help you identify a mistake at the earliest possible opportunity. If the number of stitches you've crocheted doesn't match the number at the end of the row on the pattern, you know that you've made a mistake. It's also quite easy to crochet one stitch when you actually meant to make another, especially if you are changing between two or more in the same row.

Luckily, mistakes in crochet are easy to fix, and if you catch them early enough, they won't set you back too much at all. Here's a look at how to fix mistakes and get yourself back on track.

Fix mistakes Don't panic, frog it

01 Remove hook
When you notice that things have gone awry, take your hook out of the working loop and grab hold of the working yarn.

Did you know?
Unravelling work is called frogging because you "rip it, rip it, rip it," which sounds a bit like the noise a frog makes.

02 Unravel
Pull on the working yarn to unravel the stitches one by one. This process is also known as frogging.

03 Find the mistake
Keep pulling the working yarn until you've unravelled the mistake. Stop pulling just after you've removed it.

04 Resume
Insert your hook into the working loop and begin redoing the work you've just undone, but this time without the mistake!

Fastening off

When you've finished a project, prevent it from unravelling by fastening off.

To prevent all your hard work from going to waste and unravelling before your eyes, one of the most important steps in a project is fastening off. This incredibly simple step will lock your work in place and keep all the stitches secure. Unless otherwise stated in your pattern, always fasten off your work when you come to the end of the instructions and the piece is complete.

The next step is to weave in your ends using a yarn needle. This is really simple, as you can simply insert your needle through the crocheted stitches and hide the end. Alternatively, if you are about to join a new ball of yarn, you can simply stitch over the yarn tail as you create your new stitches, effectively hiding the loose end. It's not too complicated, and it's easy to secure your work!

Fastening off Secure your yarn to complete

01 Cut the yarn
When you've finished your project, cut the working yarn about 6" (15.2cm) from the last stitch (or longer if your pattern states). Yarn over (yo) with the tail.

02 Pull through
Pull the yarn through the loop on your hook, and keep pulling until the cut end goes through the loop.

03 Pull tight
Grab the tail and pull it tight, to close the last loop. Your stitches are secure.

Top tip

When fastening off your work, take a yarn needle and thread the end around the row below the last to secure it. If you're changing color, you can stitch over the end.

Join a new yarn

If you're making a project that will use more than one ball of yarn, you'll need to join the new yarn to your fabric as seamlessly as possible.

Often projects will use up more than one ball of yarn, and certainly in amigurumi you will use lots of different colors, which means you'll need to move from using one ball to the other. This is very easy to do and there are two methods to choose from. You can either simply drop the yarn from the first ball (before you run out) at the end of a row and pick up where you left off with the new ball, or join the yarns together with a knot or other technique. Each method has its own pros and cons, and one may be more suitable for certain projects than the other. In amigurumi, this is particularly easy because you can hide the yarn ends inside your projects when you stuff them. You can draw up the new yarn as if you were working with the previous yarn and tie them off.

Join a new yarn Make a seamless move to a new ball or color

01 The last stitch
When you think there's not enough yarn left in your current ball, or you need to change color, to complete another row, begin the last stitch of your current row with the old yarn, but stop before you reach the final step (where you would yarn over and draw through all loops on hook).

02 Pick up the new yarn
Make a yarn over (yo) with the new ball of yarn and complete the stitch. Leave at a tail of at least a 6" (15.2cm) on the new yarn.

03 Drop the old yarn
Continue crocheting with the new yarn, and drop the old yarn. You can hide the ends in the inside of your project.

Joining amigurumi

Make sure that all your pieces are firmly joined together in the final shape.

Joining your amigurumi pieces together is arguably the most important part of the pattern. You don't want the piece to be coming apart at any point once you've finished the product. It can be difficult to master making your stitching look neat and tidy, but don't worry, it's really easy to unpick and do a stitch again if you think you've done it wrong. Amigurumi is very forgiving that way!

There are a couple of techniques to pick from; firstly, there is the standard joining technique, which sees you simply put the

yarn needle through the two pieces of fabrics repeatedly to join them together. There is also such a thing as the invisible join, which sees you match up the stitches from one piece to another in order to create what appears to be a seamless final look.

You can choose whatever technique works best for you— some patterns may suggest what they recommend for your joining technique, but others will leave it down to you. In these examples, we have used a different color for the threads to show you how it should look.

Join a flat piece Secure your pieces together

01 Pin your pieces
Pin your pieces together, making sure that your attaching piece is exactly where you want it.

02 Insert your needle
Insert your needle into the piece of amigurumi that you wish to attach it to, making sure that you have your needle come up below the stitch/your flat piece.

03 Pull it tight
Make sure each of your stitches is pulled tight before moving on to the next one, and that the piece you are attaching doesn't move or shift out of place.

Top tip
Make sure you pull your stitches tight as it will hide them from the average eye, and people won't be able to tell that you've joined it at all.

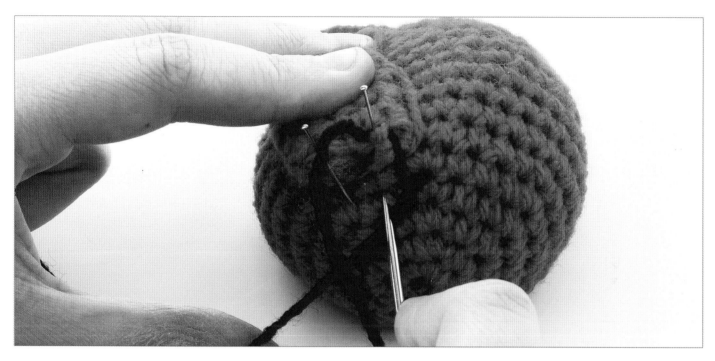

04 Go through the flat piece
Insert the needle through the flat piece, and pull the yarn through.

05 Repeat
Now keep going along the piece of edge that you want. You may find that you can see some of the stitches, but don't worry too much, that is a part of the amigurumi charm. You can make smaller stitches, or pull it tighter, if you wish to hide them.

06 Hide the end
Insert the needle into the main body of the amigurumi, then insert it to come out a stitch a few stitches down, pull it through, and then trim the end.

Getting Started

Seamless join Create a secure seamless join

01 Pin your work
You don't need to, but you may find it easier to pin your two pieces together, lining up the stitches with each other.

02 Locate the stitch
Once you have pinned your pieces (if you have opted to), you need to locate the stitch. With the piece you are joining to the flat surface, locate the V of one of the stitches—it does not matter where you begin if your piece is circular. Now look for the stitch directly below it.

03 Insert your needle
Insert the needle in the stitch directly below the stitch you are working from, take the needle along to the stitch beneath the next stitch, and then pull the yarn through. Do not pull it tight just yet.

04 Needle up
Now insert your needle from bottom to top beneath both parts of the V on the piece you are attaching.

05 Pull it tight
Now, to make the stitches "invisible," pull tight on the yarn you are working with. This creates a lovely smooth line, and makes the seam disappear from view.

Top tip
If you are attaching a limb that doesn't require you to squash the final edge, you can push your needle through the opposite side of the limb, and work your way around in the circle to secure it.

06 Keep going
Now keep going, repeating steps 3 through 5 until you reach the end of your open piece.

Pattern Gallery

Practice your new skills with these adorable amigurumi patterns

Cute turtle

Take your time with this turtle's big shell and little smile,
and he's bound to win the race for cuteness!

NAME: **AMY KEMBER**
BIO: Amy is a technical writer
living in Ottawa, Canada. Her
interest in crochet began when
she discovered an amigurumi
book in a used bookstore. After
making a pig, she was instantly
hooked. Since 2010, Amy has
been designing and selling her
own amigurumi patterns on
Etsy.
www.etsy.com/shop/
AmysGurumis/

DIFFICULTY:
★ ★ ★ ☆ ☆

HOOK
F/5 (3.75mm)

YARN
In this project, we have used
Bernat Handicrafter Cotton.
You will need to use DK weight
yarn in your chosen colors.
Color 1: Head and limbs
(2 balls)
Color 2: Body (1 ball)
Color 3: Shell (1 ball)

NOTIONS
Yarn needle
Fiberfill
1 pair 10mm oval safety eyes
Black yarn

MEASUREMENTS
9½" (24.1cm) tall

APPROX TIME TAKEN
10 hours

CUTE TURTLE

HEAD
Using the hook and col 1, make a magic ring.
Rnd 1: 6 sc into ring and pull it closed. (6 sts)
Rnd 2: 2 sc in each sc. (12 sts)
Rnd 3: (1 sc in next sc, 2 sc in next sc) 6 times.
(18 sts)
Rnd 4: (1 sc in each of next 2 sc, 2 sc in next sc) 6 times. (24 sts)
Rnd 5: (1 sc in each of next 3 sc, 2 sc in next sc) 6 times. (30 sts)
Rnd 6: (1 sc in each of next 4 sc, 2 sc in next sc) 6 times. (36 sts)
Rnd 7: (1 sc in each of next 5 sc, 2 sc in next sc) 6 times. (42 sts)
Rnds 8–12: 1 sc in each sc. (5 Rnds of 42 sts)
Rnd 13: 1 ss in each sc. (42 sts)
Rnd 14: (1 sc in each of next 6 sc, 2 sc in next sc) 6 times. (48 sts)

Rnd 15: (1 sc in each of next 7 sc, 2 sc in next sc) 6 times. (54 sts)
Rnd 16: (1 sc in each of next 8 sc, 2 sc in next sc) 6 times. (60 sts)
Rnds 17–21: 1 sc in each sc. (5 Rnds of 60 sts)
Rnd 22: (1 sc in each of next 8 sc, sc2tog over next 2 sts) 6 times. (54 sts)
Rnd 23: (1 sc in each of next 7 sc, sc2tog over next 2 sts) 6 times. (48 sts)
Rnd 24: (1 sc in each of next 6 sc, sc2tog over next 2 sts) 6 times. (42 sts)
Rnd 25: (1 sc in each of next 5 sc, sc2tog over next 2 sts) 6 times. (36 sts)
Rnd 26: (1 sc in each of next 4 sc, sc2tog over next 2 sts) 6 times. (30 sts)
Rnd 27: (1 sc in each of next 3 sc, sc2tog over next 2 sts) 6 times. (24 sts)
Fasten off.

BODY

Using col 2, make a magic ring.
Rnd 1: 6 sc into ring and pull it closed. (6 sts)
Rnd 2: 2 sc in each sc. (12 sts)
Rnd 3: (1 sc in next sc, 2 sc in next sc) 6 times. (18 sts)
Rnd 4: (1 sc in each of next 2 sc, 2 sc in next sc) 6 times. (24 sts)
Rnd 5: (1 sc in each of next 3 sc, 2 sc in next sc) 6 times. (30 sts)
Rnd 6: (1 sc in each of next 4 sc, 2 sc in next sc) 6 times. (36 sts)
Rnd 7: (1 sc in each of next 5 sc, 2 sc in next sc) 6 times. (42 sts)
Rnd 8: (1 sc in each of next 6 sc, 2 sc in next sc) 6 times. (48 sts)
Rnds 9–18: 1 sc in each sc. (10 Rnds of 48 sts)
Rnd 19: (1 sc in each of next 6 sc, sc2tog over next 2 sts) 6 times. (42 sts)
Rnd 20: 1 sc in each sc.
Rnd 21: (1 sc in each of next 5 sc, sc2tog over next 2 sts) 6 times. (36 sts)
Rnd 22: 1 sc in each sc.
Rnd 23: (1 sc in each of next 4 sc, sc2tog over next 2 sts) 6 times. (30 sts)
Rnd 24: 1 sc in each sc. (30 sts)
Fasten off.

ARMS (MAKE 2)

Using col 1, make a magic ring.
Rnd 1: 6 sc into ring and pull it closed. (6 sts)
Rnd 2: 2 sc in each sc. (12 sts)
Rnds 3–8: 1 sc in each sc. (6 Rnds of 12 sts)
Fasten off.

LEGS (MAKE 2)

Using col 1, make a magic ring.
Rnd 1: 6 sc into ring and pull it closed. (6 sts)
Rnd 2: 2 sc in each sc. (12 sts)
Rnd 3: (1 sc in next sc, 2 sc in next sc) 6 times. (18 sts)
Rnd 4: (1 sc in each of next 2 sc, 2 sc in next sc) 6 times. (24 sts)
Rnds 5–7: 1 sc in each sc. (3 Rnds of 24 sts)
Rnd 8: (1 sc in each of next 2 sc, sc2tog over next 2 sts) 6 times. (18 sts)
Fasten off.

SHELL

Col 3, make a magic ring.
Rnd 1: 6 sc into ring and pull it closed. (6 sts)
Rnd 2: 2 sc in each sc. (12 sts)
Rnd 3: (1 sc in next sc, 2 sc in next sc) 6 times. (18 sts)
Rnd 4: (1 sc in each of next 2 sc, 2 sc in next sc) 6 times. (24 sts)
Rnd 5: (1 sc in each of next 3 sc, 2 sc in next sc) 6 times. (30 sts)
Rnd 6: (1 sc in each of next 4 sc, 2 sc in next sc) 6 times. (36 sts)
Rnd 7: (1 sc in each of next 5 sc, 2 sc in next sc) 6 times. (42 sts)
Rnds 8–11: 1 sc in each sc. (4 Rnds of 42 sts)
Rnd 12: (1 sc in each of next 5 sc, sc2tog over next 2 sts) 6 times. (36 sts)
Rnd 13: 1 sc in front loops only in each sc. (36 sts)
Rnd 14: 3 dc in each sc. (108 sts)
Rnd 15: 1 hdc in each dc. (108 sts)
Fasten off.

FINISHING

ASSEMBLE THE FACE

Insert the oval safety eyes between Rnd 11 and Rnd 12 of the head and position them 4 sts apart.
Embroider a mouth on Rnd 21 using the yarn needle and black yarn.
Stuff the head firmly.

ASSEMBLE THE BODY

Stuff the body, arms, legs, and shell.
Sew the body to the head.

Note: There is one extra decrease Rnd on the head than on the body, so the last Rnd of the body (Rnd 24) should be sewn around the second to last Rnd on the head (Rnd 26).

Sew the arms to the body between Rnd 19 and Rnd 22, and position them 6 sts apart in the front.
Sew the legs to the body between Rnd 6 and Rnd 10, and position them 3 sts apart in the front.
Sew the shell to the back of the body between Rnd 9 and Rnd 21 using the back loops on Rnd 13 of the shell.

Top tip!

You can change the expression on your turtle's face simply by moving where you embroider the details. We've gone for happy and cute! Try this with any project!

Teddy bear

Create a sweet companion in the form of a teddy bear with this quick and easy project that would make a perfect baby gift!

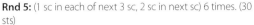

NAME: **AMY KEMBER**

BIO: Amy is a technical writer living in Ottawa, Canada. Her interest in crochet began when she discovered an amigurumi book in a used bookstore. After making a pig, she was instantly hooked. Since 2010, Amy has been designing and selling her own amigurumi patterns on Etsy.
www.etsy.com/shop/
AmysGurumis/

DIFFICULTY:
★ ★ ☆ ☆ ☆

HOOK
F/5 (3.75mm)

YARN
In this project, we have used Bernat Handicrafter Cotton. You will need to use DK weight yarn in your chosen color. Color: Skin (1 ball)

NOTIONS
1 pair 6mm safety eyes
Yarn needle
Fiberfill
Brown yarn

MEASUREMENTS
9" (22.9cm) tall

APPROX TIME TAKEN
4 hours

TEDDY BEAR

HEAD
Using the hook, make a magic ring.
Rnd 1: 6 sc into ring and pull it closed. (6 sts)
Rnd 2: 2 sc in each sc. (12 sts)
Rnd 3: (1 sc in next sc, 2 sc in next sc) 6 times. (18 sts)
Rnd 4: 1 sc in each sc. (18 sts)
Rnd 5: (1 sc in each of next 2 sc, 2 sc in next sc) 6 times. (24 sts)
Rnd 6: (1 sc in each of next 3 sc, 2 sc in next sc) 6 times. (30 sts)
Rnd 7: (1 sc in each of next 4 sc, 2 sc in next sc) 6 times. (36 sts)
Rnds 8–11: 1 sc in each sc. (4 Rnds of 36 sts)
Rnd 12: (1 sc in each of next 4 sc, sc2tog in next 2 sc) 6 times. (30 sts)
Rnd 13: (1 sc in each of next 3 sc, sc2tog in next 2 sc) 6 times. (24 sts)
Rnd 14: (1 sc in each of next 2 sc, sc2tog in next 2 sc) 6 times. (18 sts)

ASSEMBLE THE FACE
Insert the safety eyes between Rnd 1 and Rnd 2 of the head and position them 4 sts apart from each other. Embroider a nose and mouth between the eyes on the magic loop and Rnd 1 using a yarn needle and brown yarn.
Stuff the head firmly.

Rnd 15: (1 sc in next sc, sc2tog in next 2 sc) 6 times. (12 sts)
Rnd 16: (sc2tog in next 2 sc) 6 times. (6 sts)
Rnd 17: (sc2tog in next 2 sc) 3 times. (3 sts)
Hook the yarn and pull through these 3 sts to close. Fasten off.

BODY
Make a magic ring.
Rnd 1: Work 6 sc into ring and pull it closed. (6 sts)
Rnd 2: 2 sc in each sc. (12 sts)
Rnd 3: (1 sc in next sc, 2 sc in next sc) 6 times. (18 sts)
Rnd 4: (1 sc in each of next 2 sc, 2 sc in next sc) 6 times. (24 sts)

Rnd 5: (1 sc in each of next 3 sc, 2 sc in next sc) 6 times. (30 sts)
Rnds 6–13: 1 sc in each sc. (8 Rnds of 30 sts)
Rnd 14: (1 sc in each of next 3 sc, sc2tog in next 2 sc) 6 times. (24 sts)
Rnd 15: 1 sc in each sc. (24 sts)
Rnd 16: (1 sc in each of next 2 sc, sc2tog in next 2 sc) 6 times. (18 sts)
Fasten off.

EARS (MAKE 2)
Make a magic ring.
Rnd 1: 6 sc into ring and pull it closed. (6 sts)
Rnds 2–3: 1 sc in each sc. (2 Rnds of 6 sts)
Fasten off.

ARMS (MAKE 2)
Make a magic ring.
Rnd 1: 5 sc into ring and pull it closed. (5 sts)
Rnd 2: 2 sc in each sc. (10 sts)
Rnd 3–12: 1 sc in each sc. (10 rnds of 10 sts)
Fasten off.

LEGS (MAKE 2)
Make a magic ring.
Rnd 1: 8 sc into ring and pull it closed. (8 sts)
Rnd 2: 2 sc in each sc. (16 sts)
Rnd 3: 1 sc in each sc. (16 sts)
Rnd 4: 1 dc in each of next 6 sc, 1 sc in each of next 10 sc. (16 sts)
Rnd 5: (sc2tog in next 2 dc) 3 times, 1 sc in each of next 10 sc. (13 sts)
Rnds 6–13: 1 sc in each sc. (8 Rnds of 13 sts)
Fasten off.

FINISHING

Stuff the body, arms, and legs.
Sew the body to the head.
Sew the arms to the body between Rnd 15 and Rnd 16, and position them 6 sts apart in the front.
Sew the legs flat to the bottom of the body between Rnd 2 and Rnd 4, and position them close together in the front.

Little dress-up doll

Little dress-up doll's head, body, and legs are crocheted as one piece so there are fewer pieces to assemble.

NAME: **AMY KEMBER**
BIO: Amy is a technical writer living in Ottawa, Canada. Her interest in crochet began when she discovered an amigurumi book in a used bookstore. After making a pig, she was instantly hooked. Since 2010, Amy has been designing and selling her own amigurumi patterns on Etsy.
www.etsy.com/shop/AmysGurumis

DIFFICULTY:
★ ★ ★ ★ ☆

HOOK
D/3 (3.25mm)

YARN
In this project, we have used Bernat Handicrafter Cotton. You will need to use worsted weight yarn in your chosen colors.
Color 1: Skin (2 balls of yarn)
Color 2: Hair (1 ball of yarn)
Color 3: Dress (1 ball of yarn)
Color 4: Shoes (scrap yarn)

NOTIONS
1 pair 6mm safety eyes
Yarn needle
Fiberfill
Black yarn

MEASUREMENTS
8 ¾" (22.2cm) tall

APPROX TIME TAKEN
12 hours

LITTLE DRESS-UP DOLL

HEAD, BODY, AND LEGS
Using the hook and col 1, make a magic ring.
Rnd 1: 6 sc into the ring and pull it closed. (6 sts)
Rnd 2: 2 sc in each sc. (12 sts)
Rnd 3: (1 sc in next sc, 2 sc in next sc) 6 times. (18 sts)
Rnd 4: (1 sc in each of next 2 sc, 2 sc in next sc) 6 times. (24 sts)
Rnd 5: (1 sc in each of next 3 sc, 2 sc in next sc) 6 times. (30 sts)
Rnds 6–13: 1 sc in each sc. (8 Rnds of 30 sts)
Rnd 14: (1 sc in each of next 3 sc, sc2tog in next 2 sc) 6 times. (24 sts)
Rnd 15: (1 sc in each of next 2 sc, sc2tog in next 2 sc) 6 times. (18 sts)

ASSEMBLE THE FACE
Insert the safety eyes between Rnd 9 and Rnd 10 of the head and position them 3 stitches apart.
Embroider a mouth between the eyes on Rnd 12 and Rnd 13 using a yarn needle and black yarn.
Stuff the head firmly.

Rnd 16: (1 sc in next sc, sc2tog in next 2 sc) 6 times. (12 sts)
Rnd 17: (sc2tog in next 2 sc) 6 times. (6 sts)
Rnd 18: 2 sc in each sc. (12 sts)
Rnd 19: (1 sc in next sc, 2 sc in next sc) 6 times. (18 sts)
Rnd 20: (1 sc in each of next 2 sc, 2 sc in next sc) 6 times. (24 sts)
Rnds 21–32: 1 sc in each sc. (12 Rnds of 24 sts)
Stuff the body firmly.

MAKE THE LEGS
Insert the hook in the 12th sc of Rnd 32 and join with ss to separate the body into two sections for the legs (adjust the sc that you insert the hook into to make sure that the space where the body divides lines up with the eyes and mouth in the middle of the head).

Leg 1; Rnds 1–14: 1 sc in each sc around the 1st half of the body to form the 1st leg. (14 Rnds of 12 sts).
Fasten off.

Insert crochet hook into a sc on the 2nd leg opening.
Leg 2; Rnds 1–14: 1 sc in each sc around the 2nd half of the body to form the 2nd leg. (14 Rnds of 12 sts)
Stuff the legs firmly.

EARS (MAKE 2)
Using col 1, make a magic ring.
Work 6 sc into ring and pull it closed. Fasten off.

ARMS (MAKE 2)
Using col 1, make a magic ring.
Rnd 1: 4 sc into ring and pull it closed. (4 sts)
Rnd 2: 2 sc in each sc. (8 sts)
Rnds 3–5: 1 sc in each sc. (3 Rnds of 8 sts)
Rnd 6: (sc2tog in next 2 sc) 4 times. (4 sts)
Rnd 7: 2 sc in each sc. (8 sts)
Rnds 8–19: 1 sc in each sc. (12 Rnds of 8 sts)
Fasten off.

FEET (MAKE 2)

Using col 1, make a magic ring.

Rnd 1: 6 sc into ring and pull it closed. (6 sts)

Rnd 2: 2 sc in each sc. (12 sts)

Rnd 3: (2 sc in each of next 3 sc, 1 sc in each of next 3 sc) 2 times. (18 sts)

Rnd 4: 1 dc in each of next 10 sc, 1 sc in each of next 8 sc. (18 sts)

Rnd 5: (sc2tog in next 2 dc) 5 times, 1 sc in each of next 8 sc. (13 sts)

Fasten off.

HAIR (MAKE 2)

Using col 2, make a magic ring.

Rnd 1: 6 sc into ring and pull it closed. (6 sts)

Rnd 2: 2 sc in each sc. (12 sts)

Rnd 3: (1 sc in next sc, 2 sc in next sc) 6 times. (18 sts)

Rnd 4: (1 sc in each of next 2 sc, 2 sc in next sc) 6 times. (24 sts)

Rnd 5 (transition from rnds to rows): (1 sc in each of next 3 sc, 2 sc in next sc) 6 times, turn. (30 sts)

Row 6: ch 1, 1 sc in each of next 10 sc, 1 dc in each of next 10 sc, turn. (20 sts, leaving 10 sc unworked)

Row 7: ch 1, 1 dc in each of next 10 dc, 1 sc in each of next 10 sc, turn. (20 sts)

Row 8: ch 1, 1 sc in each of next 10 sc, 1 dc in each of next dc, turn. (20 sts)

Rows 9–11: ch 1, 1 sc in each st, turn. (3 Rows of 20 sts)

FORM CURLS

Row 12 (form curls): *ch 16, begin with 2nd ch from hook, 1 ss in each of next 15 ch, skip 1 sc, ss in next sc (one curl formed); repeat from * to last st, ch 16, begin with 2nd ch from hook, 1 ss in each of next 15 ch, ss in next sc. (10 curls made)

Fasten off leaving a long tail.

DRESS

Using col 3, ch 21.

Row 1: 1 sc into 2nd ch from hook, 1 sc in each ch to end, turn. (20 sts)

Row 2: ch 1, (1 sc in each of next 3 sc, 2 sc in next sc) 4 times, 1 sc in each of next 4 sc, turn. (24 sts)

Row 3: ch 1, (1 sc in each of next 4 sc, 2 sc in next sc) 4 times, 1 sc in each of next 4 sc, turn. (28 sts)

Row 4: ch 1, (1 sc in each of next 5 sc, 2 sc in next sc) 4 times, 1 sc in each of next 4 sc, turn. (32 sts)

Row 5: ch 1, (1 sc in each of next 6 sc, 2 sc in next sc) 4 times, 1 sc in each of next 4 sc, turn. (36 sts)

Row 6: ch 1, 1 sc in each sc, turn. (36 sts)

MAKE SLEEVES

Rnd 7 (transition from rows to rnds): ch 1, 1 sc in each of next 5 sc, 2 ch, skip 7 sc, join in 13th sc with ss, 1 sc in each of next 10 sc, 2 ch, skip 7 sc, join in 31st sc with ss, 1 sc in each of next 5 sc, join with ss and begin working in rnds. (24 sts)

NOTE: Do not count the slip sts from this Rnd as sts in the following rnd)

Rnds 8–11: 1 sc in each sc. (4 Rnds of 24 sts)

Rnd 12: (1 dc in next sc, 2 dc in next sc) 12 times. (36 sts)

Rnds 13–15: 1 dc in each dc. (3 Rnds of 36 sts)

Rnd 16: 1 dc in each dc to last 3 sts, 1 hdc, 1 sc, ss into last sc. (avoids jog at join)

Fasten off.

ASSEMBLE THE DRESS

To finish off the dress, ch 3 and ss into the 1st st at the top of the dress (to form the buttonhole), then continue to ss along the opening of the dress until you reach the opposite side of the opening and fasten off.

Using the other yarn end on the left side of the dress opening and a yarn needle, fasten a white button to the dress and weave in the ends.

SHOES (MAKE 2)

Using col 4, make a magic ring.

Rnd 1: 6 sc into ring and pull it closed. (6 sts)

Rnd 2: 2 sc in each sc. (12 sts)

Rnd 3: (2 sc in each of next 3 sc, 1 sc in each of next 3 sc) twice. (18 sts)

Rnd 4: 1 dc in each of next 10 sc, 1 sc in each of next 8 sc. (18 sts)

Rnd 5: (sc2tog in next 2 dc) 5 times, 1 sc in each of next 8 sc, do not fasten off. (13 sts)

MAKE SHOE STRAP

Ch 5, skip 4 sc, join in 5th sc with ss.

Fasten off.

FINISHING

Stuff the arms and feet.

Sew the hair to the head (stitch up the side of the head, along the front, down the other side of the head, and then in between the hair piece and the curls along the back).

Sew the ears to the head.

Sew the arms to the body between Rnd 19 and Rnd 20 and position them eight stitches apart in the front.

Sew the feet to the bottom of the legs.

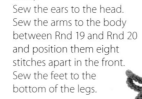

Baby sloth

This darling critter loves hanging around!
With tiny magnets in its paws, your baby sloth can hang just about anywhere!

NAME: **JASMIN WANG**
BIO: Jasmin is an artist and crafter who enjoys illustrating, painting, sewing, origami, and, of course, crocheting! She loves bringing figures, ideas, and other concepts to life through the art of crochet. Jasmin also enjoys spending time with her husband in their American Pacific Northwest home. www.etsy.com/shop/Sylemn, www.facebook.com/SweetSofties

DIFFICULTY:
★ ★ ★ ☆ ☆

HOOK
D/3 (3.25mm)

YARN
In this project, we have used Vanna's Choice by Lion Brand. You will need to use DK weighted yarn in your chosen colors.
Color 1: Body (1 ball)
Color 2: Paws (scrap yarn)
Color 3: Bow (scrap yarn)

NOTIONS
1 pair 12mm safety eyes
Dark brown or black embroidery thread
Beige and dark brown felt
Yarn needle
Embroidery needle
Fiberfill
Four 12mm neodymium magnets

MEASUREMENTS
4 ½" (11.4cm) tall

APPROX TIME TAKEN
4 hours

BABY SLOTH

HEAD AND BODY
Using the hook and col 1, make a magic ring.
Rnd 1: 6 sc in magic ring, join with ss. (6 sts)
Rnd 2: ch 1, 2 sc in each sc around, join with ss. (12 sts)
Rnd 3: ch 1, (1 sc in next sc, 2 sc in next sc) 6 times, join with ss. (18 sts)
Rnd 4: ch 1, (1 sc in each of next 2 sc, 2 sc in next sc) 6 times, join with ss. (24 sts)
Rnd 5: ch 1, (1 sc in each of next 3 sc, 2 sc in next sc) 6 times, join with ss. (30 sts)
Rnds 6–10: ch 1, sc around, join with ss. (30 sts)
Rnd 11: ch 1, (1 sc in each of next 3 sc, sc2tog) 6 times, join with ss. (24 sts)
Rnd 12: ch 1, (1 sc in each of next 6 sc, sc2tog) 3 times, join with ss. (21 sts)
Rnd 13: ch 1, sc around, join with ss. (21 sts)
Rnd 14: ch 1, (1 sc in each of next 6 sc, 2 sc in next sc) 3 times, join with ss. (24 sts)
Rnd 15: ch 1, sc around, join with ss. (24 sts)
Do not fasten off.

FACE
Using the pattern below (or your own), cut out one face from beige felt and two eye patches from dark brown felt. Make a hole in the eye patch by poking through it with a yarn needle, or cutting small X slits with scissors. The holes will be for inserting plastic safety eyes.
Mark the eye location on the face, and make holes for fitting the plastic safety eyes.
Position the face over the sloth's head. Make sure the tips of the safety eyes can be completely inserted.

NOTE: We have placed the face between Rnd 6 and Rnd 14. The eyes were positioned between Rnd 10 and Rnd 11.

Using the blanket stitch, sew the face onto the sloth. Secure the safety eyes onto the sloth.

BODY (CONT)
Continue crocheting the sloth's body.
Rnd 16: ch 1, (1 sc in each of next 7 sc, 2 sc in next sc) 3 times, join with ss. (27 sts)
Rnd 17: ch 1, (1 sc in each of next 8 sc, 2 sc in next sc) 3 times, join with ss. (30 sts)
Rnd 18: ch 1, (1 sc in each of next 9 sc, 2 sc in next sc) 3 times, join with ss. (33 sts)
Rnds 19–20: ch 1, sc around, join. (33 sts)
Rnd 21: ch 1, (1 sc in each of next 9 sc, sc2tog) 3 times, join with ss. (30 sts)
Rnd 22: ch 1, (1 sc in each of next 8 sc, sc2tog) 3 times, join with ss. (27 sts)
Rnd 23: ch 1, (1 sc in each of next 7 sc, sc2tog) 3 times, join with ss. (24 sts)
Do not fasten off yet.

Begin stuffing the head and upper body firmly, but do not stretch the stitches.
Rnd 24: ch 1, (1 sc in each of next 2 sc, sc2tog) 6 times, join with ss. (18 sts)

Rnd 25: ch 1, (1 sc in next sc, sc2tog) 6 times, join with ss. (12 sts)
Do not fasten off yet.
Finish stuffing the body.
Rnd 26: ch 1, sc2tog around, join with ss. (6 sts)
Fasten off with a long tail, and stitch the bottom closed.

ARMS (MAKE 2)
Using col 2, make a magic ring.
Rnd 1: 6 sc in magic ring, join. (6 sts)
Rnd 2: ch 1, 1 sc in each of next 3 sc, 2 sc in next sc, 1 sc in each of next 2 sc, join with ss. (7 sts)
Rnds 3–4: ch 1, sc around, join with ss. (7 sts)
Change to col 1.
Rnds 5–7: ch 1, sc around, join with ss. (7 sts)
Do not fasten off yet. Push one magnet into the hand. Keep it in place by stitching through both layers of the hand using beige yarn.
Rnds 8–20: ch 1, sc around, join with ss. (7 sts)
Fasten off, leaving a long tail for attaching to the body.

LEGS (MAKE 2)
Follow the instructions for Rnds 1–18 of the arms. The legs are two rows shorter than the arms. Do not go to Rnd 20.

BOW
Using col 3, ch 5.
Rnd 1: 1 tr into 5th ch from hook (counts as ch 4 and 1 tr), (3 tr, ch 4 , ss, ch 4, 4 tr, ch 4, ss) all into same ch.
Fasten off with a long tail for wrapping around the center of the bow. Weave in the ends.

FINISHING

Position the arms and legs on the sloth's body. Make sure the magnets in the two hands and two feet stick together. Using a yarn needle, sew the pieces to the sloth's body. Using brown yarn or embroidery thread, sew three lines over each paw.
Lastly, take the bow and sew it onto the sloth's head.

TEMPLATE

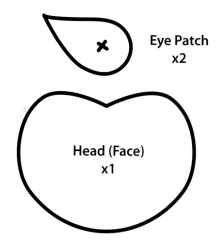

Eye Patch
x2

Head (Face)
x1

Prairie bunny

Have fun crocheting a collection of prairie bunnies
with brightly colored bonnets and coordinating fabrics inside the ears!

NAME: AMY KEMBER
BIO: Amy is a technical writer living in Ottawa, Canada. Her interest in crochet began when she discovered an amigurumi book in a used bookstore. After making a pig, she was instantly hooked. Since 2010, Amy has been designing and selling her own amigurumi patterns on Etsy.
www.etsy.com/shop/
AmysGurumis/

DIFFICULTY:
★ ★ ★ ☆ ☆

HOOK
F/5 (3.75mm)

YARN
In this project, we have used Bernat Handicrafter Cotton. You will need to use DK weight yarn in your chosen colors.
Color 1: Skin (2 balls)
Color 2: Bonnet (1 ball)

NOTIONS
1 pair 9mm safety eyes
Yarn needle
Fiberfill
Pink and cream felt
Hot glue gun
Fabric for ears
Small pom-pom for tail

MEASUREMENTS
8¼" (21cm) tall

APPROX TIME TAKEN
6 hours

PRAIRIE BUNNY

HEAD
Using the hook and col 1, make a magic ring.
Rnd 1: 6 sc into ring and pull it closed. (6 sts)
Rnd 2: 2 sc in each sc. (12 sts)
Rnd 3: (1 sc in next sc, 2 sc in the next sc) 6 times. (18 sts)
Rnd 4: (1 sc in each of next 2 sc, 2 sc in next sc) 6 times. (24 sts)
Rnd 5: (1 sc in each of next 3 sc, 2 sc in next sc) 6 times. (30 sts)
Rnd 6: (1 sc in each of next 4 sc, 2 sc in next sc) 6 times. (36 sts)
Rnd 7: (1 sc in each of next 5 sc, 2 sc in next sc) 6 times. (42 sts)
Rnd 8: (1 sc in each of next 6 sc, 2 sc in next sc) 6 times. (48 sts)
Rnds 9–16: 1 sc in each sc. (8 Rnds of 48 sts)
Rnd 17: (1 sc in each of next 6 sc, sc2tog in next 2 sc) 6 times. (42 sts)
Rnd 18: (1 sc in each of next 5 sc, sc2tog in next 2 sc) 6 times. (36 sts)
Rnd 19: (1 sc in each of next 4 sc, sc2tog in next 2 sc) 6 times. (30 sts)
Rnd 20: (1 sc in each of next 3 sc, sc2tog in next 2 sc) 6 times. (24 sts)
Rnd 21: (1 sc in each of next 2 sc, sc2tog in next 2 sc) 6 times. (18 sts)
Rnd 22: (1 sc in next sc, sc2tog in next 2 sc) 6 times. (12 sts)
Fasten off.

BODY
Using col 1, make a magic ring.
Rnd 1: 6 sc into ring and pull it closed. (6 sts)
Rnd 2: 2 sc in each sc. (12 sts)
Rnd 3: (1 sc in next sc, 2 sc in next sc) 6 times. (18 sts)
Rnd 4: (1 sc in each of next 2 sc, 2 sc in next sc) 6 times. (24 sts)
Rnd 5: (1 sc in each of next 3 sc, 2 sc in next sc) 6 times. (30 sts)
Rnd 6: (1 sc in each of next 4 sc, 2 sc in next sc) 6 times. (36 sts)
Rnds 7–12: 1 sc in each sc. (6 Rnds of 36 sts)

Rnd 13: (1 sc in each of next 4 sc, sc2tog in next 2 sc) 6 times. (30 sts)
Rnd 14: (1 sc in each of next 3 sc, sc2tog in next 2 sc) 6 times. (24 sts)
Rnd 15: (1 sc in each of next 2 sc, sc2tog in next 2 sc) 6 times. (18 sts)
Fasten off.

EARS (MAKE 2)
Using col 1, make a magic ring.
Rnd 1: 6 sc into ring and pull it closed. (6 sts)
Rnd 2: 2 sc in each sc. (12 sts)
Rnd 3: (1 sc in next sc, 2 sc in next sc) 6 times. (18 sts)

Rnd 4: (1 sc in each of next 2 sc, 2 sc in next sc) 6 times. (24 sts)
Rnd 5: 1 sc in each sc. (24 sts)
Fasten off.

ARMS (MAKE 2)

Using col 1, make a magic ring.
Rnd 1: 6 sc into ring and pull it closed. (6 sts)
Rnd 2: 2 sc in each sc. (12 sts)
Rnds 3–8: 1 sc in each sc. (6 Rnds of 12 sts)
Rnd 9: sc2tog 6 times. (6 sts)
Fasten off.

LEGS (MAKE 2)

Using col 1, make a magic ring.
Rnd 1: 6 sc into ring and pull it closed. (6 sts)
Rnd 2: 2 sc in each sc. (12 sts)
Rnd 3: (1 sc in next sc, 2 sc in next sc) 6 times. (18 sts)
Rnds 4–5: 1 sc in each sc. (2 Rnds of 18 sts)
Rnd 6: (1 sc in next sc, sc2tog in next 2 sc) 6 times. (12 sts)
Fasten off.

SUNBONNET

Using col 2, make a magic ring.
Rnd 1: 6 sc into ring and pull it closed. (6 sts)
Rnd 2: 2 sc in each sc. (12 sts)
Rnd 3: (1 sc in next sc, 2 sc in next sc) 6 times. (18 sts)
Rnd 4: (1 sc in each of next 2 sc, 2 sc in next sc) 6 times. (24 sts)
Rnd 5: (1 sc in each of next 3 sc, 2 sc in next sc) 6 times. (30 sts)
Rnd 6: (1 sc in each of next 4 sc, 2 sc in next sc) 6 times. (36 sts)
Rnd 7: (1 sc in each of next 5 sc, 2 sc in next sc) 6 times. (42 sts)
Rnd 8: (1 sc in each of next 6 sc, 2 sc in next sc) 6 times. (48 sts)
Rnds 9–10: 1 sc in each sc. (2 Rnds of 48 sts)
Turn and begin working in rows.
Row 11: ch 1, 1 sc in each of next 42 sc leaving 6 sc unworked for the neck opening, turn. (42 sts)
Rows 12–14: ch 1, 1 sc in each sc, turn. (3 rows of 42 sts)

Row 15 (make opening for ears): ch 1, 1 sc in each of next 15 sc, ch 6, skip 5 sc, join in 21st sc with ss, ch 6, skip 5 sc, join in 27th sc with ss, 1 sc in each of next 15 sc, turn. (42 sts—do not count slip sts from this Rnd as sts in the following rnd)
Row 16: ch 1, 1 sc in each sc, turn. (42 sts)
Row 17: ch 1, 1 ss in each sc, turn. (42 sts)
Row 18: ch 1, (1 dc in each of next 2 ss, 2 dc in next ss) 13 times, 1 dc in each of the next 3 sc, turn. (55 sts)
Row 19: ch 1, 1 dc in each dc, turn. (55 sts)
Row 20 (make ties for sunbonnet): ch 21, beginning with 2nd ch from hook, 1 ss in each of next 20 ch, ss evenly across the bottom neckline of the sunbonnet, ch 21, beginning with 2nd ch from hook, 1 ss in each of next 20 ch.
Fasten off and weave in ends.

ASSEMBLE THE FACE

Insert the safety eyes between Rnd 13 and Rnd 14 of the head and position them six stitches apart.
Stuff the head firmly.
Cut out a pink felt nose and a cream felt muzzle to the shape of your choice.
Glue the nose to the muzzle using a hot glue gun.
Position the muzzle and nose between the eyes but slightly higher up on the face between Rnd 11 and Rnd 16.
Glue the muzzle and nose to the prairie bunny's face using a hot glue gun.

FINISHING

Stuff the body, arms, and legs.
Sew the body to the head—there is one extra decrease Rnd on the head than on the body so the last Rnd of the body (Rnd 15) should be sewn around the second to last Rnd on the head (Rnd 21).
Sew the arms to the body between Rnd 14 and Rnd 15 and position them six stitches apart in the front.
Sew the legs to the body between Rnd 6 and Rnd 8 and position them two stitches apart in the front.
Cut out two fabric circles that will fit into the ears as shown. Glue the fabric inside each crocheted ear using a hot glue gun.
Place the sunbonnet on the prairie bunny's head to determine the position of the ears (so they can poke through the ear openings in the sunbonnet).
Before sewing an ear to the head, take the yarn tail of the ear and, using a yarn needle, skip three stitches from the tail and thread the tail through the fourth stitch, pulling it tight to shape the ear.
Only a few stitches are required to sew the ear to the prairie bunny, threading the needle through the same area where the four stitches were gathered together in order to fasten it to the head.
Glue a pom-pom to the prairie bunny's lower back between Rnd 5 and Rnd 6 of the body using a hot glue gun.

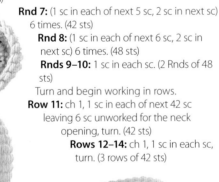

Tiny princess

Create princesses, flower girls, or bridesmaids that are quick to make, easily customizable, and serve as lovely handmade gifts.

NAME: **JASMIN WANG**

BIO: Jasmin is an artist and crafter who enjoys illustrating, painting, sewing, origami and, of course, crocheting! She loves bringing figures, ideas, and other concepts to life through the art of crochet. Jasmin also enjoys spending time with her husband in their American Pacific Northwest home. www.etsy.com/shop/Sylemn, www.facebook.com/ SweetSofties

DIFFICULTY:
★ ★ ★ ☆ ☆

HOOK
D/3 (3.25mm)

YARN
In this project, we have used Caron's Simply Soft. You will need to use DK weight yarn in your chosen colors.
Color 1: Skin (1 ball)
Color 2: Dress (1 ball)
Color 3: Hair (1 ball)

NOTIONS
1 pair 6mm safety eyes
Embroidery thread
Yarn needle
Fiberfill
Beads/pellets for weighted stuffing in the body
Rose & ribbon

MEASUREMENTS
3 ¾" (9.5cm) tall

APPROX TIME TAKEN
3 hours

TINY PRINCESS

HEAD
Using the hook and col 1, make a magic ring.
Rnd 1: 6 sc in magic ring, join with ss. (6 sts)
Rnd 2: ch 1, 2 sc in each sc, join with ss. (12 sts)
Rnd 3: ch 1, (1 sc in next sc, 2 sc in next sc) 6 times, join with ss. (18 sts)
Rnd 4: ch 1, (1 sc in each of next 2 sc, 2 sc in next sc) 6 times, join with ss. (24 sts)
Rnds 5–9: ch 1, 1 sc around, join with ss. (5 Rnds of 24 sts)
Rnd 10: ch 1, (1 sc in each of next 2 sc, sc2tog) 6 times, join with ss. (18 sts)
Rnd 11: ch 1, (1 sc in next sc, sc2tog) 6 times, join with ss. (12 sts)
Fasten off.
Stuff the head firmly, but be careful not to stretch sts.

HAIR CAP
Using col 3, make a magic ring.
Complete as for Rnds 1–8 of head, then fasten off leaving a long tail for attaching to head later.

HAIR BUN
Using col 3, make a magic ring.
Rnd 1: 6 sc in magic ring, join with ss. (6 sts)
Rnd 2: ch 1, 2 sc in each sc around, join with ss. (12 sts)
Rnd 3: ch 1, (1 sc in next 3 sc, 2 sc in next sc) 3 times, join with ss. (15 sts)
Rnds 4–5: ch 1, sc around, join with ss. (2 Rnds of 15 sts)
Change to col 2 to create a contrasting hair tie/ribbon.
Rnd 6: ch 1, (1 sc in next 3 sc, sc2tog) 3 times, join with ss. (12 sts)
Fasten off, leaving a long tail for attaching to the hair cap later.

BODY
Using col 2, make a magic ring.
Rnd 1: 6 sc in magic ring, join with ss. (6 sts)
Rnd 2: ch 1, 2 sc in each sc around, join with ss. (12 sts)
Rnd 3: ch 1, (1 sc in next sc, 2 sc in next sc) 6 times, join with ss. (18 sts)
Rnd 4 (blo): ch 1, 1 sc in each sc, join with ss. (18 sts)
Rnd 5–6: ch 1, sc around, join with ss. (2 rnds of 18 sts)
Rnd 7: ch 1, (1 sc in each of next 7 sc, sc2tog) twice, join with ss. (16 sts)
Rnd 8: ch 1, 1 sc in each sc, join with ss. (16 sts)
Rnd 9: ch 1, (1 sc in each of next 6 sc, sc2tog) twice, join with ss. (14 sts)
Rnd 10: ch 1, 1 sc in each sc, join with ss. (14 sts)
Rnd 11: ch 1, (1 sc in each of next 5 sc, sc2tog) twice, join with ss. (12 sts)
Rnd 12: ch 1, 1 sc in each sc, join with ss. (12 sts)
Fasten off, leaving a long tail for attaching to the head later.

Note: When stuffing the body, add some beads/pellets to the bottom to provide some weight and stability, then stuff the rest of the body with fiberfill stuffing.

DRESS
Note: Dress is attached to the body.
Hold the body upside down (with the neck opening facing down).

Using col 2, attach the yarn to the starting st on the bottom of the princess's body at Rnd 9.

Rnd 1: ch 1, sc around, join with ss. (14 sts)
Rnd 2: 3 ch, (1 dc in each of next 6 dc, 2 dc in next dc) twice, join with ss. (16 sts)
Rnd 3: 3 ch, (1 dc in each of next 3 dc, 2 dc in next dc) 4 times, join with ss. (20 sts)
Rnd 4 (scalloped edging): ch 1, *1 sc in next dc, (1 hdc, 1 dc) in next dc, (1 dc, 1 hdc) in next dc, 1 sc in next dc; rep from * 5 times, join with ss. (5 scallops made)
Fasten off, and weave in ends.

ARMS (MAKE 2)
Using col 1, ch 8.
1 sc into 2nd ch from hook, 1 sc into each ch to end. (7 sc)
Fasten off with tail for attaching.

FINISHING

Attach the pair of plastic safety eyes to the head (we put them between Rnd 7 and Rnd 8, 4 sts apart).
Using an embroidery needle and red/pink thread, sew a mouth onto the doll's face.
Using black thread, sew eyelashes to the corners of the eyes.
Stuff the hair bun lightly. Place the hair bun over the hair cap, and sew it on using a yarn needle. Then place the hair cap over the doll's head and sew it on. Attach your rose ribbon with a needle and thread.

Note: See the wedding doll pattern on page 142 for different hairstyle ideas for your tiny princess.

Sew the arms onto the body, then sew the head firmly onto the body.
Fasten off.

Rob the raptor

Rob is a friendly, chubby raptor who would rather keep you company than chase smaller dinosaurs. Rob is made with basic stitches and just a little bit of yarn!

NAME: **SARAH SLOYER**

BIO: When Sarah Sloyer first discovered amigurumi, she became determined to teach herself how to crochet so she could make them! After lots of practice, she is finally designing and writing her own patterns, which she loves sharing with others.
www.ravelry.com/stores/critterbeans

DIFFICULTY:
★ ★ ★ ☆ ☆

HOOK
D/3 (3.25mm)

YARN
In this project, we have used Lion Brand yarn. You will need medium weight yarn in your chosen colors.
Color 1: Body (1 ball)
Color 2: Stripes (scrap yarn)

NOTIONS
1 pair 6mm safety eyes
Fiberfill
Scissors
Stitch markers
Yarn needle

MEASUREMENTS
4¼" (10.8cm) tall

APPROX TIME TAKEN
7 hours

SPECIAL STITCH USED
Cluster (see page 159)

ROB THE RAPTOR

HEAD AND BODY
Using the hook and col 1, ch 5.
Rnd 1 (RS): 1 sc in 2nd ch from hook, 1 sc in next 2 ch, 4 sc in last ch, rotate and work along opposite side of foundation ch, 1 sc in next 2 sts, 4 sc in next st. You now have a small oval. Place marker in next st (this will be the first st of next round). (13 sts)
Rnd 2: 1 sc in next 4 sts, 3 sc in next st, 2 sc in next st, 1 sc in next 4 sts, 2 sc in next 3 sts. (19 sts)
Rnd 3: (1 sc in next 2 sts, 2 sc in next st) 6 times, 1 sc in next st. (25 sts)
Rnd 4: 1 sc in next 2 sts, 2 sc in next st, (1 sc in next 4 sts, 2 sc in next st) 4 times, 1 sc in next 2 sts. (30 sts)
Rnd 5: 1 sc in next 7 sts, (2 sc in next st, 1 sc in next st) 5 times, 1 sc in next 13 sts. (35 sts)
Rnd 6: 1 sc in next 8 sts, (2 sc in next st, 1 sc in next st) 6 times, 1 sc in next 6 sts changing to col 2 on last yo of 6th sc, 1 sc in next 5 sts, 2 sc in next st, 1 sc in next 3 sts. (42 sts)
Rnd 7: 1 sc in first st changing to col 1 on last yo of st, 1 sc in next 31 sts, 1 sc in next st changing to col 2 on last yo of st, 1 sc in next 9 sts.
Rnd 8: 1 sc in first st changing to col 1 on last yo of st, 1 sc in remaining 41 sts.
Rnd 9: 1 sc in next 29 sts, 2 sc in next st, 1 sc in next 2 sts, 2 sc in next st, (1 sc in next 3 sts, 2 sc in next st) twice, 1 sc in next st. (46 sts)
Rnd 10: (1 sc in next 2 sts, 2 sc in next st) twice, 1 sc in next 6 sts, sc2tog, 1 sc in next 8 sts, sc2tog, 1 sc in next 22 sts. (48 sts)
Rnd 11: 1 sc in next 18 sts, sc2tog, 1 sc in next 11 sts, 2 sc in next st, 1 sc in next 2 sts, 1 sc in next st changing to col 2 on last yo of st, 1 sc in next st, 2 sc in next st, 1 sc in next 4 sts, 2 sc in next st, 1 sc in next 4 sts. (48 sts)

Place the safety eyes between Rnds 2 and 3 on the right, and Rnds 3 and 4 on the right.

Rnd 12: 2 sc in first st, 1 sc in next st, 1 sc in next st changing to col 1 on last yo of st, 1 sc in next 4 sts, 2 sc in next st, 1 sc in next 5 sts, sc2tog, 1 sc in next 7 sts, sc2tog, 1 sc in next 10 sts, 1 sc in next st changing to col 2 on last yo of st, 1 sc in next 13 sts. (48 sts)
Rnd 13: 1 sc in next 3 sts, 1 sc in next st changing to col 1 on last yo of st, 1 sc in next 10 sts, sc2tog, 1 sc in next 7 sts, sc2tog, 1 sc in next 7 sts, 2 sc in next st, (1 sc in next 5 sts, 2 sc in next st) twice, 1 sc in next 3 sts. (49 sts)

Rnd 14: 1 sc in next 2 sts, 2 sc in next st, 1 sc in next 5 sts, 2 sc in next st, 1 sc in next 5 sts, sc2tog, 1 sc in next 6 sts, sc2tog, 1 sc in next 25 sts. (49 sts)
Rnd 15: 1 sc in next 16 sts, sc2tog, 1 sc in next 4 sts, sc2tog, 1 sc in next 9 sts, 2 sc in next st, (1 sc in next 4 sts, 2 sc in next st) 3 times. (51 sts)
Rnd 16: 1 sc in next 7 sts, 2 sc in next st, 1 sc in next 7 sts, (sc2tog) 5 times, 1 sc in next 3 sts, 2 sc in next st, 1 sc in next 4 sts, 2 sc in next st changing to col 2 on last yo of in second st of inc, (1 sc in next 4 sts, 2 sc in next st) 3 times, 1 sc in next 2 sts. (52 sts)
Rnd 17: 1 sc in next 2 sts, 2 sc in next st, 1 sc in next 2 sts, 1 sc in next st changing to col 1 on last yo of st, 1 sc in next st, 2 sc in next st, 1 sc in next 4 sts, 2 sc in next st, 1 sc in next 3 sts, (sc2tog) 3 times, 1 sc in next 9 sts, 1 sc in next st changing to col 2 on last yo of st, 1 sc in next 20 sts. (52 sts)
Rnd 18: 1 sc in next 6 sts, 1 sc in next st changing to col 1 on last yo of st, 1 sc in next 11 sts, (sc2tog) twice, 1 sc in next 30 sts. (50 sts)
Rnd 19: (1 sc in next 9 sts, 2 sc in next st) 5 times. (55 sts)
Rnd 20: 1 sc in each st. (55 sts)
Rnd 21: 1 sc in next 5 sts, 2 sc in next st, (1 sc in next 10 sts, 2 sc in next st) 4 times, 1 sc in next 5 sts. (60 sts)
Rnds 22–23: 1 sc in each st. (2 Rnds of 60 sts)
Rnd 24: (1 sc in next 9 sts, 2 sc in next st) 6 times. (66 sts)

Did you know?
The word "crochet" is derived from the Middle French word *croc* or *croche*, meaning "hook."

Rnds 25–26: 1 sc in each st. (2 Rnds of 66 sts)
Rnd 27: (1 sc in next 9 sts, sc2tog) 6 times. (60 sts)
Stuff the head generously, then continue. Don't stuff the body yet.
Rnd 28: 1 sc in next 4 sts, sc2tog, (1 sc in next 8 sts, sc2tog) 5 times, 1 sc in next 4 sts. (54 sts)
Rnd 29: (1 sc in next 7 sts, sc2tog) 6 times. (48 sts)
Rnd 30: 1 sc in next 3 sts, sc2tog, (1 sc in next 6 sts, sc2tog) 5 times, 1 sc in next 3 sts. (42 sts)
Rnd 31: (1 sc in next 5 sts, sc2tog) 6 times. (36 sts)
Rnd 32: 1 sc in next 2 sts, sc2tog, (1 sc in next 4 sts, sc2tog) 5 times, 1 sc in next 2 sts. (30 sts)
Begin stuffing the body generously as you work the following rounds.
Rnd 33: (1 sc in next 3 sts, sc2tog) 6 times. (24 sts)
Rnd 34: 1 sc in next st, sc2tog, (1 sc in next 2 sts, sc2tog) 5 times, 1 sc in next st. (18 sts)
Rnd 35: (1 sc in next st, sc2tog) 6 times. (12 sts)
Rnd 36: (sc2tog) 6 times. (6 sts)
ss in next st and fasten off. Close hole by threading your tail through the front loops of the remaining 6 sts, then pulling tight. Weave in tail.

TAIL

In col 2, make a magic loop.
Rnd 1 (RS): 5 sc in magic loop. (5 sts)
Rnd 2: (2 sc in next st, 1 sc in next st) twice, 2 sc in next st. (8 sts)
Change to col 1.
Rnd 3: (2 sc in next st, 1 sc in next st) 3 times, 1 sc in next 2 sts. (11 sts)
Rnd 4: 1 sc in each st. (11 sts)
Rnd 5: 1 sc in next 2 sts, 2 sc in next st, (1 sc in next 3 sts, 2 sc in next st) twice. (14 sts)
Change to col 2.
Rnd 6: 1 sc in each st. (14 sts)
Rnd 7: 1 sc in next 3 sts, 2 sc in next st, (1 sc in next 4 sts, 2 sc in next st) twice. (17 sts)
Change to col 1.
Rnd 8: 1 sc in each st. (17 sts)
Rnd 9: 1 sc in next 4 sts, 2 sc in next st, (1 sc in next 5 sts, 2 sc in next st) twice. (20 sts)
Rnd 10: 1 sc in each st. (20 sts)
Change to col 2.
Rnd 11: (1 sc in next 3 sts, 2 sc in next st) 5 times. (25 sts)
Rnd 12: 1 sc in each st. (25 sts)
Fasten off with a slip stitch and leave a tail for sewing.

ARMS (MAKE 2)

Note: The stitches can get quite tight while making the arms, so you can size your hook up if it makes it easier for you.

Using col 1, make a magic loop
Rnd 1 (RS): 5 sc in magic loop. (5 sts)
Rnds 2–5: 1 sc in each st. (4 Rnds of 5 sts)
Do not fasten off or stuff the arm. Press the arm flat and 1 sc in next 2 sts across top of arm, through both sides, to close it. Yarn over and pull through to fasten off, leaving a tail for sewing.

LEGS (MAKE 2)

Using col 1, make a magic loop.
Rnd 1 (RS): 5 sc in magic loop. (5 sts)
Rnd 2: 2 sc in each st. (10 sts)
Rnd 3: (1 sc in next st, 2 sc in next st) 5 times. (15 sts)
Rnd 4: 1 sc in next st, (1 cluster in next st, 1 sc in next st) 3 times, 1 sc in next 8 sts. (15 sts)

Note: The cluster stitches from Rnd 4 make it harder to see the stitches in this round. Be careful not to miss any in Rnd 5.

Rnd 5: 1 sc in each st. (15 sts)
Rnd 6: (1 sc in next 3 sts, sc2tog) 3 times. (12 sts)
Rnd 7: 1 sc in each st. (12 sts)
ss in next st and fasten off, leaving a long tail for sewing.

FINISHING

TAIL ASSEMBLY

Stuff the tail lightly, then pin and sew it to the body. Add more stuffing as you go.

ARMS ASSEMBLY

Starting from the bottom of the body, count 15 to 16 rounds up and insert your yarn needle into body, and then insert the yarn needle into one of the two stitches on the top of the arm. Reinsert the needle into the body at the same place where you originally inserted your needle before. Repeat a few times until secure then move onto the second stitch on top of the arm and repeat until secure. Count approximately seven stitches along then repeat the same steps with the next arm.

LEGS ASSEMBLY

Stuff the legs lightly and pin them to your raptor, then sew them to the body using your leftover yarn tail. Tip: Set your raptor on a flat surface while you pin the legs to the body to ensure that it will sit correctly.

Happy horse

Design a horse that has a playful and floppy head,
and is able to stand on his four hooves or sit on his back legs.

NAME: **AMY KEMBER**
BIO: Amy is a technical writer living in Ottawa, Canada. Her interest in crochet began when she discovered an amigurumi book in a used bookstore. After making a pig, she was instantly hooked. Since 2010, Amy has been designing and selling her own amigurumi patterns on Etsy.
www.etsy.com/shop/
AmysGurumis/

DIFFICULTY:
★ ★ ★ ★ ☆

HOOK
F/5 (3.75mm)

YARN
In this project, we have used Bernat Handicrafter Cotton. You will need to use DK weight yarn in your chosen colors.
Color 1: Skin (2 balls)
Color 2: Mane (1 ball)
Color 3: Hooves (1 ball)

NOTIONS
1 pair 6mm safety eyes
Yarn needle
Fiberfill
Black yarn scraps to embroider mouth and nose

MEASUREMENTS
8¾" (22.2cm) tall (when sitting on back legs)

APPROX TIME TAKEN
10 hours

HAPPY HORSE

HEAD
Using the hook and col 1, make a magic ring.
Rnd 1: 6 sc into ring and pull it closed. (6 sts)
Rnd 2: 2 sc in each sc. (12 sts)
Rnd 3: (1 sc in next sc, 2 sc in next sc) 6 times. (18 sts)
Rnd 4: (1 sc in each of next 2 sc, 2 sc in next sc) 6 times. (24 sts)
Rnds 5–16: 1 sc in each sc. (12 Rnds of 24 sts)

ASSEMBLE THE FACE
Insert the safety eyes between Rnd 12 and Rnd 13 of the head and position them 6 sts apart from each other.
Embroider a nose (two nostrils) between Rnd 2 and Rnd 3 using a yarn needle and black yarn.
Embroider a mouth along 9 sts between Rnd 3 and Rnd 4. Stuff the head firmly.
Rnd 17: (1 sc in each of next 2 sc, sc2tog in next 2 sc) 6 times. (18 sts)
Rnd 18: (1 sc in next sc, sc2tog in next 2 sc) 6 times. (12 sts)
Finish stuffing the head firmly before fastening off.

BODY
Using col 1, make a magic ring.
Rnd 1: 6 sc into ring and pull it closed. (6 sts)
Rnd 2: 2 sc in each sc. (12 sts)
Rnd 3: (1 sc in next sc, 2 sc in next sc) 6 times. (18 sts)
Rnd 4: (1 sc in each of next 2 sc, 2 sc in next sc) 6 times. (24 sts)
Rnd 5: (1 sc in each of next 3 sc, 2 sc in next sc) 6 times. (30 sts)
Rnds 6–21: 1 sc in each sc. (16 Rnds of 30 sts)
Rnd 22: 1 sc in each of next 6 sc, 1 dc in each of next 24 sc. (30 sts)
Rnd 23: 1 sc in each of next 6 sc, (sc2tog in next 2 dc) 12 times. (18 sts)
Rnd 24: 1 sc in each of next 6 sc, 1 dc in each of next 12 sc. (18 sts)
Begin stuffing the body.
Rnd 25: 1 sc in each of next 6 sc, (sc2tog in next 2 dc) 6 times. (12 sts)
Rnd 26: 1 sc in each of next 6 sc, 1 dc in each of next 6 sc. (12 sts)
Rnds 27–36: sc in each st. (10 Rnds of 12 sts)
Finish stuffing the body firmly before fastening off.

EARS (MAKE 2)
Using col 1, make a magic ring.
Rnd 1: 4 sc into ring and pull it closed. (4 sts)
Rnds 2–4: 1 sc in each sc. (3 Rnds of 4 sts)
Fasten off.

LEGS (MAKE 4)
Using col 3, make a magic ring.
Rnd 1: 6 sc into ring and pull it closed. (6 sts)
Rnd 2: 2 sc in each sc. (12 sts)
Rnd 3 (blo): 1 sc in each sc. (12 sts)
Rnd 4: 1 sc in each sc. (12 sts)
Change to col 1.

Rnd 5 (blo): 1 sc in each sc. (12 sts)
Rnds 6–22: 1 sc in each sc. (17 Rnds of 12 sts)
Fasten off.

FINISHING

Stuff the legs.
Join the head to the neck of the body: using the yarn tail from the head, holding both pieces squeezed flat along tops while crocheting them together, 6 sc straight across through all four thicknesses to join as one piece.
Sew the ears to the head between Rnd 16 and Rnd 17.
Sew two of the legs to the bottom of the body between Rnd 6 and Rnd 9, and position them 2 sts apart.
Sew the other two legs to the bottom of the body between Rnd 18 and Rnd 21, and position them 2 sts apart.

ASSEMBLE THE MANE
Cut twenty-seven 6" (15.2cm) strands of col 2.
Fold a strand in half; insert crochet hook into a st on the top of the horse's neck, then insert the hook into the center of a folded strand; pull the strand up through the st in the neck to form a loop; pull the two ends of the strand through the loop to secure the strand.
Repeat until you have 12 strands on each side of the horse's neck between Rnd 24 and Rnd 36.
Attach three strands using this method to the front of the head to form the forelock and trim the ends.

ASSEMBLE THE TAIL
Cut twenty 11¾" (29.8cm) strands of col 2.
Tie the strands together with another strand in the center. Tie this tassel to the end of the horse's body (between Rnd 2 and Rnd 3) for the tail.

Rachel doll

This project is perfect for trying out your skills in miniature to produce a doll full of fun and character.

NAME: **KATRINA EVANS**
BIO: Katrina enjoys creating lifelike miniatures with character and style. She has developed a special interest in custom-made crocheted pets from photos, her greyhounds and whippets have proved especially popular and have been ordered by customers in the UK and Europe.
www.etsy.com/uk/shop/KatyJaneCreations

DIFFICULTY:
★ ★ ★ ☆ ☆

HOOK
B/1 (2mm)

YARN
In this project, we have used King Cole 4-ply bamboo.
You will need to use super fine weight yarn in your chosen colors.
Color 1: Skin (1 ball)
Color 2: Shoes (scrap yarn)
Color 3: Hair (scrap yarn)
Color 4: Shirt (scrap yarn)
Color 5: Skirt (scrap yarn)
Color 6: Vest (scrap yarn)
Color 7: Bag and vest edges (scrap yarn)

NOTIONS
Yarn needle
Fiberfill
Black yarn

MEASUREMENTS
Approx 7" (17.8cm) tall depending on hook and yarn size used

APPROX TIME TAKEN
8 hours

RACHEL DOLL

HEAD
Using the hook and col 1, make a magic ring.
Rnd 1: 6 sc into the ring and pull it closed. (6 sts)
Rnd 2: 2 sc in each sc. (12 sts)
Rnd 3: (1 sc in next sc, 2 sc in next sc) 6 times. (18 sts)
Rnd 4: (1 sc in each of next 2 sc, 2 sc in next sc) 6 times. (24 sts)
Rnd 5: (1 sc in each of next 3 sc, 2 sc in next sc) 6 times. (30 sts)
Rnds 6–13: 1 sc in each sc. (8 Rnds of 30 sts)
Rnd 14: (1 sc in each of next 3 sc, sc2tog in next 2 sc) 6 times. (24 sts)
Rnd 15: (1 sc in each of next 2 sc, sc2tog in next 2 sc) 6 times. (18 sts)
Lightly stuff the head.
Rnd 16: (1 sc in next sc, sc2tog in next 2 sc) 6 times. (12 sts)
Rnd 17: (1 sc in next 2 sc, sc2tog in next 2 sc) 3 times. (9 sts)
Rnd 18: 1 sc in each sc. (9 sts)
Fasten off.

LEGS
FIRST LEG
Using col 2, make ch 5.
Rnd 1: 2 sc into 2nd ch from hook, 1 sc in each of next 2 ch, 4 sc in next ch, rotate work to cont along bottom of ch, 1 sc in each of next 2 ch, 4 sc in next ch. (14 sts)
Rnd 2: 2 sc in next sc, 1 sc in each of next 3 sc, 2 hdc in each of next 4 sc, 1 sc in each of next 3 sc, 2 sc in each of next 3 sc. (22 sts)
You should now be at the heel of the foot.
Rnd 3: 1 sc in each sc. (22 sts)
Rnd 4: 1 sc in each of next 7 sc, (sc2tog in next 2 sc) 4 times, 1 sc in each of next 7 sc. (18 sts)
Change to col 1.
Rnd 5 (flo): 1 sc in each of next 5 sc, (sc2tog in next 2 sc) 4 times, 1 sc in each of next 5 sc. (14 sts)
Rnd 6: 1 sc in each of next 5 sc, (sc2tog in next 2 sc) twice, 1 sc in each of next 5 sc. (12sts)
Stuff the foot and continue on to leg.
Rnd 7: 1 sc in each of next 4 sc, (sc2tog in next 2 sc) twice, 1 sc in each of next 4 sc. (10 sts)
Rnd 8: 1 sc in each of next 3 sc, (sc2tog in next 2 sc) twice, 1 sc in each of next 3 sc. (8 sts)
Rnds 9–17: 1 sc in each sc. (9 Rnds of 8 sts)

Stuff lower leg lightly.
Rnd 18: (sc2tog in next 2 sc) twice, 1 sc in next sc, 2 sc in each of next 2 sc, 1 sc in next sc. (8 sts)
Rnd 19: 1 sc In each of next 4 sc, 1 hdc in each of next 4 sc. (8 sts)
Rnd 20: 1 sc in each st. (8 sts)
Rnd 21: 1 sc in each of next 6 sc, 2 sc in next sc, 1 sc in next sc. (9 sts)
Rnd 22: 1 sc in each of next 6 sc, 2 sc in next sc, 1 sc in each of next 2 sc. (10 sts)
Rnds 23–32: 1 sc in each sc. (10 Rnds of 10 sts)
Fasten off, adding more stuffing if needed, then twist the leg a little until foot and knee are facing the same direction.

SECOND LEG
Work Rnds 1–32 as for first leg but do not fasten off, and do not trim your working yarn tail.
Stuff both legs, then hold the first leg next to the second in position, making sure the knees are facing the same way, with the feet toward you. Make sure the yarn is on the far right side of the doll by your right hand, still on the second leg.

JOIN LEGS TOGETHER
Rnd 33: With legs held side by side and squeezed flat along tops, ch 1, 1 sc in each sc straight across first leg through two thicknesses, then continue across other leg to join as one piece, turn. (10 sts—5 sts for each leg)
Rnd 34: ch 1, 1 sc in each of next 10 sc along the back loops, then turn and continue working 1 sc in each of next 10 sc in front loops. (20 sts)
Rnd 35: 1 sc in each sc. (20 sts)
Rnd 36: 1 sc in each of next 2 sc, 2 sc in next sc, (1 sc in next sc, 2 sc in next sc) 3 times, 1 sc in each of next 11 sc. (24 sts)
Rnds 37–40: 1 sc in each sc. (4 Rnds of 24 sts)
Rnd 41: 1 sc in each of next 4 sc, sc2tog in next 2 sc, 1 sc in each of next 2 sc, (sc2tog in next 2 sc) twice, 1 sc in each of next 2 sc, sc2tog in next 2 sc, 1 sc in each of next 8 sc. (20 sts)
Rnd 42: 1 sc in each sc. (20 sts)
Rnd 43: (1 sc in each of next 3 sc, sc2tog in next 2 sc) 4 times. (16 sts)
Rnds 44–52: 1 sc in each sc. (9 Rnds of 16 sts)
Rnd 53: 1 sc in each of next 3 sc, (sc2tog in next 2 sc) 3 times, 1 sc in next sc, (sc2tog in next 2 sc) 3 times. (10 sts)
Start to stuff the body.

Rnd 54: (1 sc in each of next 3 sc, sc2tog in next 2 sc) twice. (8 sts)

Rnds 55–57: 1 sc in each sc. (3 Rnds of 8 sts)

Fasten off, then add a little more stuffing into the neck. Use a sewing needle and yarn to carefully sew on the head, catching alternate stitches from the head and neck.

ARMS (MAKE 2)

Using col 1, make a magic ring.

Rnd 1: 4 sc into the ring and pull it closed, leaving 7cm tail (later to become thumb). (4 sts)

Rnd 2: 2 sc in each sc. (8sts)

Rnds 3–4: 1 sc in each sc. (2 Rnds of 8 sts)

Rnd 5: sc2tog in next 2 sc, 1 sc in each of next 6 sc. (7 sts)

Rnd 6: sc2tog in next 2 sc, 1 sc in each of next 5 sc. (6 sts)

Rnds 7–14: 1 sc in each sc. (8 Rnds of 6 sts)

Rnd 15: sc2tog in next 2 sc, 1 sc in next sc, 2 sc in next sc, 1 sc in next sc. (6 sts)

Rnd 16: 1 sc in each of next 3 sc, 1 hdc in next 3 sc. (6 sts)

Rnd 17: 1 sc in next sc, 2 sc in next sc, 1 sc in next sc, 1 sc in each of next 4 hdc. (7 sts)

Rnds 18–25: 1 sc in each sc. (8 Rnds of 7 sts)

Stuff the arms lightly and sew them closed with a needle. Insert the hook in a thumb position on the hand, out through the end of the hand and pull back the tail. Insert the hook into the same hole and out through the adjoining hole, then pull through the tail to form a loop, ch 2, then fasten off. Pull the end of the tail back through the same hole, leaving the thumb sticking out and use the hook to hide the rest of the tail inside the arm. Sew the arms to the body.

WIG CAP, HAIR, AND FACE

Using col 3, work Rnds 1–5 as for head. (30 sts)

Rnds 6–10: 1 sc in each sc. (5 Rnds of 30 sts)

Rnd 11: (1 sc in each of next 4 sc, 2 sc in next sc) 6 times. (36 sts)

Rnd 12: 1 sc in each sc. (36 sts)

Fasten off. This is the basis for the wig cap.

Sew the cap at a slight angle to the back/top of the head, catching stitches all around the edges of the cap, but not too tight so as to distort the head shape.

Next, embroider a simple face. If you are using the 4-ply bamboo yarn, you will find it splits easily into separate threads ideal for embroidery.

Using col 3, make a chain long enough to stretch like a hair part from the top front of the head to the top of the neck—this will form the chain to attach the hair.

Sew this to the wig cap from the middle of the forehead to the nape of the neck.

Stitch a few strands of wool from the edge of the cap onto her forehead to give her a fringe.

Measure a strand of wool from the crocheted chain down to the length of hair as you would like it, and double the strand. Cut several strands of this length and start attaching these strands individually to the center chain with your hook—insert the hook into a chain space, catch a loop mid-length of the doubled strand, pull it partway through, and then insert the two loose ends through the loop, pulling tight. Continue in this way until you have completed the length of the chain.

Alternatively, experiment with different styles by cutting lots of strands of similar length and weaving them randomly into the cap using the above method. Ensure you cover the edges of the cap. You may find this easier if you use a smaller hook. This is your chance to personalize and stylize your doll and use your creative skills!

When the hair is as thick as you want, trim and style the hair, but don't make it too short, otherwise the strands might pull through.

TOP AND UNDERWEAR

Using col 4 make 27 ch.

Row 1: 1 sc in 2nd ch from hook, 1 sc in each sc to end, turn. (26 sts)

Row 2: ch 1, 1 sc in each of next 5 sc, ch 5, skip 5 sc, 1 sc in each of next 6 sc, ch 5, skip 5 sc, 1 sc in each of next 5 sc, turn. (26 sts)

Row 3: ch 1, 1 sc in each of next 5 sc, 5 sc in ch–sp, 1 sc in each of next 6 sc, 5 sc in ch–sp, 1 sc in each of next 5 sc, turn. (26 sts)

Rows 4–8: ch 1, 1 sc in each sc, turn. (26 sts and 26 ch-sps)

Join with ss and continue to work in rnds.

Rnds 9–15: 1 sc in each sc. (7 Rnds of 26 sts)

Rnd 16 (flo): ch 3, (skip next st, ss in next st) 13 times. (13 sts)

Rnd 16 (blo): 1 sc in each of next 26 sc. (13 sts—26 sts total)

Rnd 17–20: 1 sc in each sc. (4 rnds of 26)

Place top on doll, work two to three more sc to end at the center and ss to join between the legs to create underwear.

Fasten off, leaving long tail. Thread the tail onto a needle and pull it up inside the top on the doll, sewing up the back of the neck seam. Adjust the shoulder straps and sew them in place on the doll if you like.

SKIRT

Using col 5, ch 24 and, without twisting chain, join to make a circle.

Rnd 1: ch 2 (does not count as st), 1 dc in each ch. (24 sts).

Rnds 2–5: ch 2 (does not count as st), 1 dc in each dc. (24 sts).

Fasten off and leave a long end.

Pull the skirt onto the doll, use the tail to weave through to waistline, and then stitch the skirt invisibly to the waist.

VEST

Using col 6, ch 17.

Row 1: 1 sc into 2nd ch from hook, 1 sc in each of next 15 sc. (16 sts)

Row 2: ch 1, 1 sc in each sc, turn. (16 sts)

Row 3: ch 1, (1 sc in next sc, 2 sc in next sc) 8 times, turn. (24 sts)

Row 4: ch 1, 1 sc in each of next 2 sc, ch 5, skip next 5 sc, 1 sc in each of next 4 sc, 2 sc in each of next 2 sc, 1 sc in each of next 4 sc, ch 5, skip next 5 sc, 1 sc in each of next 2 sc, turn. (26 sts)

Row 5: ch 1, 1 sc in each of next 2 sc, 5 sc in ch–sp, 1 sc in each of next 12 sc, 5 sc in ch–sp, 1 sc in each of next 2 sc turn. (26 sts)

Rnd 6: ch 1, 1 sc into each sc, turn. (26 sts)

Row 7: ch 1, 1 sc in each of next 10 sc, (sc2tog in next 2 sc) 3 times, 1 sc in each of next 10 sc. (23 sts)

Fasten off.

Using col 7, join to any corner.

Rnd 8 (edging): ch 1, sc evenly around entire vest, working 2 sc in each corner, join. (27 sts)

Fasten off and weave in the tail.

BAG

Using col 7, make 8 ch.

Rnds 1: 1 sc into 2nd ch from hook, 1 sc in each of next ch 5, 3 sc in next ch, rotate work to cont along bottom of ch, 1 sc in each of next 6 ch, 3 sc in next ch. (18 sts)

Rnds 2–5: 1 sc in each sc. (4 Rnds of 18 sts)

Rnd 6 (make shoulder strap): 30 ch, skip 8 sc, join with ss in next sc, ss into next sc.

Turn and begin working in rows.

Row 1 (make bag flap): ch 1, skip st with shoulder strap attached, 1 sc in next 8 sc, turn. (8 sts)

Row 2: ch 1, sc2tog in next 2 sc, 1 sc in each of next 4 sc, sc2tog in next 2 sc. (6 sts).

Fasten off and weave in the end.

Thread the needle with another color and sew a simple cross to look like a button to close the flap of the bag. Hide the ends inside the bag.

Tiny luck elephant

Tiny luck elephant is a preciously petite project that is quick and easy to make and is the perfect gift for a child.

NAME: **MARI-LIIS LILLE**
BIO: Mari-Liis, known as lilleliis, has been crazy about amigurumi since 2008 when she first discovered crochet. Since then, designing toys has become her greatest passion and self-realization. She is the author of many pattern books published in her native language (Estonian), as well as in English, Dutch, Korean, and Spanish.
www.lilleliis.com

DIFFICULTY:
★ ★ ☆ ☆ ☆

HOOK
D/3 (3.25mm)

YARN
In this project, we have used BBB Filati Full: 100% pure new wool. You will need to use DK weight yarn in your chosen colors.
Color 1: Body (1 ball)
Color 2: Flower (yarn scraps)

NOTIONS
1 pair 6mm safety eyes
Cotton fabric
Yarn needles
Fiberfill
Two stitch markers
Embroidery thread

MEASUREMENTS
3 ½" (8.9cm) in sitting position

APPROX TIME TAKEN
6 hours

TINY LUCK ELEPHANT

HEAD
Using the hook and col 1, make a magic ring.
Rnd 1: 6 sc into ring and pull it closed. (6sts)
Rnd 2: 1 sc in each sc. (6 sts)
Rnd 3: 1 sc in each of next 2 sc, 2 sc in next sc, 1 sc in each of next 3 sc. (7 sts)
Rnd 4: 1 sc in each of next 2 sc, 2 sc in next sc, 1 sc in each of next 4 sc. (8 sts)
Rnd 5: 1 sc in each of next 2 sc, 2 sc in next sc, 1 sc in each of next 5 sc. (9 sts)
Rnd 6: 1 sc in each of next 2 sc, 2 sc in next sc, 1 sc in each of next 6 sc. (10 sts)
Rnd 7: 1 sc in each of next 2 sc, 2 sc in next sc, 1 sc in each of next 7 sc. (11 sts)
Rnd 8: 1 sc in each of next 2 sc, 2 sc in next sc, 1 sc in each of next 8 sc. (12 sts)
Rnd 9: 1 sc in each of next 2 sc, 2 sc in each of next 2 sc, 1 sc in each of next 8 sc. (14 sts)
Rnd 10: (1 sc in each of next 2 sc, 2 sc in next sc) twice, 1 sc in each of next 8 sc. (16 sts)
Rnd 11: 1 sc in next sc, 2 sc in next sc, 1 sc in each of next 8 sc, 2 sc in next sc, 1 sc in each of next 5 sc. (18 sts)
Mark the first stitch of the next round with your marker and do not move it from there as you will need it when placing the safety eyes. You can mark the beginning of the coming rounds with the second stitch marker.
Rnd 12: (1 sc in next sc, 2 sc in next sc) 6 times, 1 sc in each of next 6 sc. (24 sts)
Rnd 13: (1 sc in each of next 3 sc, 2 sc in the next sc) 6 times. (30 sts)
Rnds 14–18: 1 sc in each sc, do not fasten off. (5 Rnds of 30 sts)

Go back to Rnd 12 where you have the first stitch marked. Find the second increase in this row (the stitch where you've made 2 sc in one st) and insert the safety eye right below it. Insert the second eye below the fifth increase. You should see five stitches between the two eyes. Close the washers on the inside of the work.

Rnd 19: (1 sc in each of next 3 sc, sc2tog) 6 times. (24 sts)
Rnd 20: 1 sc in each sc. (24 sts)
Stuff the trunk and continue adding stuffing.
Rnd 21: (1 sc in each of next 2 sc, sc2tog) 6 times. (18 sts)
Rnd 22: 1 sc in each sc. (18 sts)
Rnd 23: (1 sc in next sc, sc2tog) 6 times. (12 sts)
Rnd 24: (sc2tog) 6 times. (6 sts)
Fasten off leaving a tail for closing the piece. Hook yarn through the front loops of all 6 sts on the last round and pull tight. Make a knot and weave in yarn end.

EARS (MAKE 2)
Using col 1, make a magic ring.
Rnd 1: 6 sc into ring and pull it closed. (6 sts)
Rnd 2: Work 2 sc in each sc. (12 sts)
Rnd 3: (1 sc in next sc, 2 sc in next sc) 6 times. (18 sts)
Rnd 4: (1 sc in each of next 2 sc, 2 sc in next sc) 6 times. (24 sts)
Rnd 5: (1 sc in each of next 3 sc, 2 sc in next sc) 6 times. (30 sts)
Rnd 6: 1 sc in each sc. (30 sts)

Fold the piece in half keeping your hook at the right corner. Crochet along the open edge working through both layers. Work 15 sc along the edge.
Fasten off, leaving a long tail for sewing.

ASSEMBLING THE EARS
The ears need to mirror each another and are attached from above, so bring the yarn tail of one of the ears out on the other tip of the ear.
Cut out pieces of fabric following the shape of the ears. Sew them on. Attach the ears to the head. Make only a half seam from the top to the middle of the ear (the place where you can see the starting magic ring).
Stitch the eyelashes.

BODY
Using col 1, make a magic ring.
Rnd 1: 6 sc into ring and pull it closed. (6 sts)
Rnd 2: 2 sc in each sc around. (12 sts)
Rnd 3: (1 sc in next sc, 2 sc in next sc) 6 times. (18 sts)
Rnd 4: (1 sc in each of next 2 sc, 2 sc in next sc) 6 times. (24 sts)
Rnds 5–7: 1 sc in each sc. (3 Rnds of 24 sts)
Rnd 8: (1 sc in each of next 2 sc, sc2tog) 6 times. (18 sts)
Rnds 9–12: 1 sc in each sc. (4 Rnds of 18 sts)
Rnd 13: (1 sc in the next sc, sc2tog) 6 times. (12 sts)
Fasten off, leaving a long tail for sewing. Stuff the body. Attach the head to the body.

LEGS (MAKE 2)
Using col 1, make a magic ring.
Rnd 1: 6 sc into ring and pull it closed. (6 sts)
Rnd 2: Work 2 sc in each sc. (12 sts)
Rnd 3 (blo): 1 sc in each sc. (12 sts)
Rnd 4: (1 sc in each of next 2 sc, sc2tog) 3 times. (9 sts)
Rnds 5–6: 1 sc in each sc. (2 Rnds of 9 sts)
Fasten off, leaving a long tail for sewing.
Stuff the legs.
Cut small round pieces of fabric and sew onto the soles. Attach the legs toward the front.

ARMS (MAKE 2)
Using col 1, make a magic ring.
Rnd 1: 6 sc into ring and pull it closed. (6 sts)
Rnds 2–7: 1 sc in each sc. (6 Rnds of 6 sts)
Fasten off, leaving a long tail for sewing. Attach the arms between the head and body.

TAIL
Cut a length of yarn about 15 ¾" (40cm) long and fold it in half. Bring the hook between the stitch spaces. Grab the yarn and pull up a loop. Ch 5 using both strands. Slip the yarn tail through the last stitch and pull tight. Leave a tail about ½" (1.3cm) long. Untwist the ends to give a tufty look.

FLOWER
Using col 2, make a magic ring.
(1 sc, ch 4) 5 times into ring and pull it closed, join with ss in first sc. Fasten off, leaving a long tail for sewing. Attach the flower to the elephant's head.

Proud lion

Create your own pride of adorable lions with this simple but effective pattern that will have your lion sitting on his hind legs.

NAME: **AMY KEMBER**
BIO: Amy is a technical writer living in Ottawa, Canada. Her interest in crochet began when she discovered an amigurumi book in a used bookstore. After making a pig, she was instantly hooked. Since 2010, Amy has been designing and selling her own amigurumi patterns on Etsy.
www.etsy.com/shop/
AmysGurumis

DIFFICULTY:
★ ★ ★ ☆ ☆

HOOK
F/5 (3.75mm)

YARN
In this project, we have used Bernat Handicrafter Cotton. You will need to use DK weight yarn in your chosen colors.
Color 1: Skin (2 balls)
Color 2: Paws (1 ball)
Color 3: Mane (1 ball)

NOTIONS
1 pair 10mm oval safety eyes
Yarn needle
Fiberfill
Pink and white felt
Hot glue gun

MEASUREMENTS
8¼" (21cm) tall

APPROX TIME TAKEN
9 hours

PROUD LION

HEAD
Using the hook and col 1, make a magic ring.
Rnd 1: 6 sc into ring and pull it closed. (6 sts)
Rnd 2: 2 sc in each sc. (12 sts)
Rnd 3: (1 sc in next sc, 2 sc in next sc) 6 times. (18 sts)
Rnd 4: (1 sc in each of next 2 sc, 2 sc in next sc) 6 times. (24 sts)
Rnd 5: (1 sc in each of next 3 sc, 2 sc in next sc) 6 times. (30 sts)
Rnd 6: (1 sc in each of next 4 sc, 2 sc in next sc) 6 times. (36 sts)
Rnd 7: (1 sc in each of next 5 sc, 2 sc in next sc) 6 times. (42 sts)
Rnd 8: (1 sc in each of next 6 sc, 2 sc in next sc) 6 times. (48 sts)
Rnds 9–16: 1 sc in each sc. (8 Rnds of 48 sts)
Rnd 17: (1 sc in each of next 6 sc, sc2tog in next 2 sc) 6 times. (42 sts)
Rnd 18: (1 sc in each of next 5 sc, sc2tog in next 2 sc) 6 times. (36 sts)
Rnd 19: (1 sc in each of next 4 sc, sc2tog in next 2 sc) 6 times. (30 sts)
Rnd 20: (1 sc in each of next 3 sc, sc2tog in next 2 sc) 6 times. (24 sts)
Rnd 21: (1 sc in each of next 2 sc, sc2tog in next 2 sc) 6 times. (18 sts)
Rnd 22: (1 sc in next sc, sc2tog in next 2 sc) 6 times. (12 sts)
Fasten off.

BODY
Using col 1, make a magic ring.
Rnd 1: 6 sc into ring and pull it closed. (6 sts)
Rnd 2: 2 sc in each sc. (12 sts)
Rnd 3: (1 sc in next sc, 2 sc in next sc) 6 times. (18 sts)
Rnd 4: (1 sc in each of next 2 sc, 2 sc in next sc) 6 times. (24 sts)
Rnd 5: (1 sc in each of next 3 sc, 2 sc in next sc) 6 times. (30 sts)
Rnd 6: (1 sc in each of next 4 sc, 2 sc in next sc) 6 times. (36 sts)
Rnd 7: (1 sc in each of next 5 sc, 2 sc in next sc) 6 times. (42 sts)
Rnds 8–9: 1 sc in each sc. (2 Rnds of 42 sts)

Rnd 10: (1 sc in each of next 5 sc, sc2tog in next 2 sc) 6 times. (36 sts)
Rnds 11–12: 1 sc in each sc. (2 Rnds of 36 sts)
Rnd 13: (1 sc in each of next 4 sc, sc2tog in next 2 sc) 6 times. (30 sts)
Rnds 14–17: 1 sc in each sc. (4 Rnds of 30 sts)
Rnd 18: (1 sc in each of next 3 sc, sc2tog in next 2 sc) 6 times. (24 sts)
Rnd 19: 1 sc in each sc. (24 sts)
Rnd 20: (1 sc in each of next 2 sc, sc2tog in next 2 sc) 6 times. (18 sts)
Fasten off.

EARS (MAKE 2)
Using col 1, make a magic ring.
Rnd 1: 6 sc into ring and pull it closed. (6 sts)
Rnds 2–4: 1 sc in each sc. (3 Rnds of 6 sts)
Fasten off.

FRONT LEGS (MAKE 2)
Using col 2, make a magic ring.
Rnd 1: 6 sc into ring and pull it closed. (6 sts)
Rnd 2: 2 sc in each sc. (12 sts)
Rnd 3: (1 sc in next sc, 2 sc in next sc) 6 times. (18 sts)
Rnd 4: 1 sc in each sc. (18 sts)
Rnd 5: (1 sc in next sc, sc2tog in next 2 sc) 6 times. (12 sts)
Change to col 1.
Rnd 6–11: 1 sc in each sc. (6 Rnds of 12 sts)
Rnd 12: (1 sc in next sc, sc2tog in next 2 sc) 4 times. (8 sts)
Rnds 13–17: 1 sc in each sc. (5 Rnds of 8 sts)
Fasten off.

BACK LEGS (MAKE 2)
Using col 2, make a magic ring.
Rnd 1: 6 sc into ring and pull it closed. (6 sts)
Rnd 2: 2 sc in each sc. (12 sts)
Rnd 3: (1 sc in next sc, 2 sc in next sc) 6 times. (18 sts)
Rnd 4: 1 sc in each sc. (18 sts)
Rnd 5: (1 sc in next sc, sc2tog in next 2 sc) 6 times. (12 sts)
Change to col 1.
Rnd 6–7: 1 sc in each sc. (2 Rnds of 12 sts)
Fasten off.

TAIL

Using col 3, make a magic ring.
Rnd 1: 6 sc into ring and pull it closed. (6 sts)
Rnd 2: 2 sc in each sc. (12 sts)
Change to col 1.
Rnd 2: ch 16
Fasten off and weave in ends.

MANE EDGING

Using col 3, ch 69.
Row 1: 1 sc into 2nd ch from hook, sc to end, turn.
(48 sts)
Row 2: ch 3 (counts as dc), 4 dc in first sc, skip next sc, 1 ss in next sc, (skip next sc, 5 dc in next sc, skip next sc, 1 ss in next sc) 11 times, ss in last sc. (12 scallops made)
Fasten off.

MANE

Using col 3, make a magic ring.
Rnd 1: 6 sc into ring and pull it closed. (6 sts)
Rnd 2: 2 sc in each sc. (12 sts)
Rnd 3: (1 sc in next sc, 2 sc in next sc) 6 times. (18 sts)
Rnd 4: (1 sc in each of next 2 sc, 2 sc in next sc) 6 times. (24 sts)
Rnd 5: (1 sc in each of next 3 sc, 2 sc in next sc) 6 times. (30 sts)
Rnd 6: (1 sc in each of next 4 sc, 2 sc in next sc) 6 times. (36 sts)
Rnd 7: (1 sc in each of next 5 sc, 2 sc in next sc) 6 times. (42 sts)
Rnd 8: (1 sc in each of next 6 sc, 2 sc in next sc) 6 times. (48 sts)
Rnd 9-10: 1 sc in each sc. (2 rnds of 48 sts)
Turn and begin working in rows.
Row 11: ch 1, 1 sc in each of next 42 sc, turn.
(42 sts—leaving 6 sc unworked for the neck opening)
Rows 12-14: ch 1, 1 sc in each sc, turn. (3 rows of 42 sts)
Row 15 (make opening for ears): ch 1, 1 sc in each of next 11 sc, 6 ch, skip 5 sc, join in 16th sc with ss, 1 sc in each of next 8 sc, 6 ch, skip 5 sc, join in 31st sc with ss, 1 sc in each of next 11 sc, turn. (42 sts—do not count the slip sts from this Rnd as sts in the following rnd)
Row 16: ch 1, sc in each sc. (42 sts)
Set aside while assembling the lion but do not fasten off.

ASSEMBLE THE FACE

Insert the oval safety eyes between Rnd 12 and Rnd 13 of the head and position them seven stitches apart.
Stuff the head firmly.
Cut out a pink felt nose and a white felt muzzle.
Glue the nose to the muzzle using a hot glue gun.
Position the muzzle and nose between the eyes but slightly higher up on the face between Rnd 10 and Rnd 15.
Glue the muzzle and nose to the lion's face using a hot glue gun.

FINISHING

Stuff the body, arms, and legs.
Sew the body to the head—there is one extra decrease Rnd on the head than on the body so the last Rnd of the body (Rnd 20) should be sewn around the second to last Rnd on the head (Rnd 21).
Sew the arms to the body between Rnd 16 and Rnd 18, and position them so they are four stitches apart in the front.
Sew the legs to the body between Rnd 7 and Rnd 9 and position them 15 stitches apart in the front.
Place the mane on the lion's head to determine the position of the ears (so they can poke through the ear openings in the mane).
Sew the ears to the head between Rnd 5 and Rnd 7.
To secure the mane, ch 6 across the neck and join on the other side of the mane with a slip stitch.
Sew the mane edging to the mane.
Sew the tail to the back of the body between Rnd 7 and Rnd 8.

Top tip!
Create a pride of
friends for your lion, and
leave the mane bonnet
off to create some
female friends.

Magical unicorn

Learn how to easily bring this much-loved fantasy creature
into the real world—horn and all!

NAME:

MEVLINN GUSICK

BIO: Mevlinn is a college
graduate with a BFA in Fine Arts
Painting. Her interest in knitting
and crochet began when her
aunt suggested she try knitting.
It piqued her curiosity and
here she is today, crocheting
amigurumi whenever she gets
the chance and giving them to
those she loves.
www.mevvsan.com

DIFFICULTY:
★ ★ ☆ ☆ ☆

HOOK
2.75 mm (US C/2)

YARN
In this project, we have used
Rosario 4 Catitano. You will need
medium weight yarn in your
chosen colors.
Color 1: Body (1 ball)
Color 2: Dark mane and tail color
(scrap yarn)
Color 3: Hooves (scrap yarn)
Color 4: Horn (scrap yarn)
Color 5: Light mane and tail color
(scrap yarn)

NOTIONS
1 pair 9mm safety eyes
Scissors
Stitch marker (optional)
Fiberfill
Yarn needle

MEASUREMENTS
11" (27.9cm) tall

APPROX TIME TAKE
6 hours

MAGICAL UNICORN

BODY
Using col 1, make a magic ring.
Rnd 1 (RS): 7 sc in magic ring. (7 sts)
Rnd 2: 2 sc in each st around. (14 sts)
Rnd 3: (2 sc in next st, 1 sc in next st) 7 times. (21 sts)
Rnd 4: (2 sc in next st, 1 sc in next 2 sts) 7 times. (28 sts)
Rnd 5: (2 sc in next st, 1 sc in next 3 sts) 7 times. (35 sts)
Rnd 6: (2 sc in next st, 1 sc in next 4 sts) 7 times. (42 sts)
Rnd 7: 1 sc in each st around. (42 sts)
Rnd 8: (2 sc in next st, sc in next 5 sts) 7 times. (49 sts)
Rnd 9: 1 sc in each st around. (49 sts)
Rnds 10–12: sc2tog, 1 sc in each remaining st. (46 sts after Rnd 12)
Rnds 13–14: sc2tog, 1 sc in each st to the last 3 sts, sc2tog, 1 sc in last st. (42 sts after Rnd 14)
Stuff with fiberfill and continue stuffing as you go.
Rnds 15–22: sc2tog, 1 sc in each st to the last 3 sts, sc2tog, 1 sc in last st. (26 sts after Rnd 22)
Rnds 23–28: sc2tog, 1 sc in each remaining st. (20 sts after Rnd 28)
Fasten off, leaving a tail for sewing. When the head is
complete, you will use this yarn end to sew the body and
head together.

Note: The body has a side-specific decrease. This
decrease is creating the "rump" of the unicorn. Keep this
in mind when you sew the head on later.

HEAD
Using col 1, make a magic ring.
Rnd 1 (RS): 6 sc in magic ring. (6 sts)
Rnd 2: 2 sc in each st around. (12 sts)
Rnd 3: (2 sc in next st, 1 sc in next st) 6 times. (18 sts)
Rnd 4: (2 sc in next st, 1 sc in next 2 sts) 6 times. (24 sts)
Rnd 5: (2 sc in next st, 1 sc in next 3 sts) 6 times. (30 sts)
Rnd 6: (2 sc in next st, 1 sc in next 4 sts) 6 times. (36 sts)
Rnds 7–15: 1 sc in each st around. (8 Rnds of 36 sts)
Change to col 2.
Rnd 16: (2 sc in next st, 1 sc in next 5 sts) 6 times. (42 sts)
Place the eyes between Rnds 12 and 13 with 10 sts
between the eyes.
Rnds 17–21: 1 sc in each st around. (5 Rnds of 42 sts)
Stuff with fiberfill and continue stuffing as you go.
Rnd 22: (sc2tog, 1 sc in next 5 sts) 6 times. (36 sts)
Rnd 23: (sc2tog, 1 sc in next 4 sts) 6 times. (30 sts)
Rnd 24: (sc2tog, 1 sc in next 3 sts) 6 times. (24 sts)

Rnd 25: (sc2tog, 1 sc in next 2 sts) 6 times. (18 sts)
Rnd 26: (sc2tog, 1 sc in next st) 6 times. (12 sts)
Rnd 27: (sc2tog) 6 times. (6 sts)
Fasten off, leaving a long tail for sewing. Using your yarn
needle, weave the yarn tail through the front ring of each
remaining st and pull it tight to close.
Sew the head onto the body. The back of the neck should
sew onto Rnd 6 of the head.

LEGS (MAKE 2)
Using col 3, make a magic ring.
Rnd 1: 4 sc in magic ring. (4 sts)
Rnd 2: 2 sc in each st around. (8 sts)
Rnd 3: (2 sc in next st, 1 sc in next st) 4 times. (12 sts)
Rnd 4: 1 sc in each st around. (12 sts)
Change to col 1.
Rnd 5–17: 1 sc in each st around. (13 rounds of 12 sts)
Fasten off, leaving a tail for sewing. Lightly stuff the legs
with more stuffing near the hooves.

ASSEMBLE THE LEGS
Start by sewing the back legs first. Place the unicorn on a
flat surface in the seated position you want to create, and
pin the legs to the sides of the body.
Attach the back legs at Rnds 6–8 of the body with 12 sts
between the initial attachment points of each leg. Sew
each leg about 8 sts down the leg against the body to
stop them from bowing out.

Pattern Gallery

When the hind legs are attached, the unicorn should be able to sit well on its own, and this helps when sewing the front legs. Attach the front legs at Rnd 19 of the body with 4 sts between each leg. Sew each leg about 8 sts down the leg against the body to stop the front legs from bowing out.

EARS (MAKE 2)
Using col 1, ch 5.
Row 1: 1 sc in 2nd ch from hook, 1 sc in next 2 ch, 4 sc in last ch, rotate and work along the opposite side of the foundation ch, 1 sc in next 3 ch, turn. (10 sts)
Row 2: ch 1 (not counted as a st), 1 sc in next 3 sts, 2 sc in next 4 sts, 1 sc in next 3 sts, turn. (14 sts)
Row 3: ch 1 (not counted as a st), 1 sc in each st around. (14 sts)

Fasten off, leaving a tail for sewing. Pinch the base of the ear together and sew the ears 6 Rnds behind the eyes with 9 sts between each ear.

HORN
Using col 4, make a magic ring
Rnd 1 (RS): 4 sc in magic ring. (4 sts)
Rnds 2–6 (blo): 2 sc in next st, 1 sc in each remaining st. (9 sts after Rnd 6)

Fasten off, leaving a long tail for sewing.
Sew the horn unstuffed onto the top of the head between the ears and the eyes.

TAIL
Cut five strands of col 2 that are 11¾" (29.8cm) in length and cut five strands of col 5 that are 11¾" (29.8cm) in length. Take one strand of each col and fold them in half.
With the folded end between your fingers, insert your crochet hook in the rump of your unicorn where you want the tail to be (about Rnd 8 of the body), place the folded ends of the yarn onto the hook, and pull them back through the body. Take the loose ends of the yarn, wrap them around the hook, and pull them through the rings. Pull to tighten. Repeat this four more times in sts adjacent to the first st to create a thick tail.

Separate the strands into three sections and braid them. Take a piece of col 4 and wrap it around the end of the braid, then tie it tightly with a bow.

MANE
Cut a few dozen strands each of cols 2 and 5 that are 9¾" (24.8cm) in length. Find the center of the unicorn's head and, using one strand at a time, attach the mane using the same method as given for the tail. To keep the mane straight, follow the sts down the back in a straight line until about 15 strands have been attached, alternating between col 2 and col 5. Repeat to add another line on each side of the center mane to create three lines in total. Trim and braid the mane, if desired.

Top tip!
Use different shades of the same color to create a herd of unicorns to accompany your new friend, or use glittery yarn for an added dash of magic.

Yeti & Bigfoot

With this pattern, make a cute and cuddly monster:
either a snow-dwelling Yeti or a hairy mountain Bigfoot.

NAME: **LUCY COLLIN**
BIO: Lucy has been designing amigurumi for seven years. Her children encouraged her to use her crochet skills to make them cute toys, and she then started to sell the patterns online. She has had two books published, including *Star Wars Crochet*, and has had several patterns included in various magazines. lucyravenscar.blogspot.com

DIFFICULTY:
★ ★ ★ ☆ ☆

HOOK
E/4 (3.5mm)

YARN
In this project, we have used Stylecraft Alpaca DK and Sirdar Country Style yarn. You will need DK weight yarn in your chosen colors.

Color 1: Body (1 ball)
Color 2: Face, hands, and feet (scrap yarn)

NOTIONS
1 pair 15mm safety eyes
Black yarn
Fiberfill
Wire pet brush
Yarn needle

MEASUREMENTS
9" (22.9cm) tall

APPROX TIME TAKEN
6–8 hours

SPECIAL STITCHES
Loop stitch (see page 158)
6dc popcorn stitch (6dc-pop) (see page 159)

YETI & BIGFOOT

FACE (MAKE THIS FIRST)
Using col 2, ch2.
Rnd 1: 6 sc in 2nd ch from hook. (6 sts)
Rnd 2: 2 sc in each st around. (12 sts)
Rnd 3: (2 sc in next st, 1 sc in next st) 6 times. (18 sts)
Rnd 4: *1 sc in next 3 sts, (2 sc in next st, 1 sc in next st) 3 times; rep from * once more. (24 sts)
Rnd 5: 1 sc in next 4 sts, (2 sc in next st, 1 sc in next st) 3 times, 1 sc in next 6 sts, (2 sc in next st, 1 sc in next st) 3 times, 1 sc in next 2 sts. (30 sts).
Rnd 6: 1 sc in next 6 sts, (2 sc in next st, 1 sc in next st) 3 times, 1 sc in next 9 sts, (2 sc in next st, 1 sc in next st) 3 times, 1 sc in next 3 sts. (36 sts).
Rnd 7: 1 sc in next 6 sts, (2 sc in next st, 1 sc in next 2 sts) 3 times, 1 sc in next 9 sts, (2 sc in next st, 1 sc in next 2 sts) 3 times, 1 sc in next 3 sts. (42 sts)
Rnd 8: 1 sc in next 7 sts, (2 sc in next st, 1 sc in next 3 sts) 3 times, 1 sc in next 9 sts, (2 sc in next st, 1 sc in next 3 sts) 3 times, 1 sc in next 2 sts. (48 sts)
Change to col 1.
Rnd 9: 1 sc in each st around. (48 sts)
ss in next st, ch 1, turn to make ruff with the wrong side facing you.
Rnd 10: Loop stitch in each st around (see page 158 for full details of how to do this stitch). (48 sts)
ss into first loop stitch and fasten off, leaving a long length of yarn to sew the face to the body. Next, cut the loops and, using a wire pet brush, separate the strands of yarn to make them fuzzy. If you don't have a wire pet brush you can use a needle to separate the strands, it just takes a lot longer. Trim the ruff to the length you require.

EMBROIDER THE MOUTH
Push the safety eyes through the face between Rnds 5 and 6, on either side of the center (do not attach the washers yet). Use the black yarn to embroider the mouth. Secure the end of the yarn on the back of the face before cutting it.

BODY
Using col 1, ch2.
Rnd 1: 6 sc in 2nd ch from hook. (6 sts)
Rnd 2: 2 sc in each st around. (12 sts)
Rnd 3: (2 sc in next st, 1 sc in next st) 6 times. (18 sts)
Rnd 4: (2 sc in next st, 1 sc in next 2 sts) 6 times. (24 sts)
Rnd 5: (2 sc in next st, 1 sc in next 3 sts) 6 times. (30 sts)
Rnd 6: (2 sc in next st, 1 sc in next 4 sts) 6 times. (36 sts)

Rnd 7: (2 sc in next st, 1 sc in next 5 sts) 6 times. (42 sts)
Rnd 8: (2 sc in next st, 1 sc in next 6 sts) 6 times. (48 sts)
Rnd 9: (2 sc in next st, 1 sc in next 7 sts) 6 times. (54 sts)
Rnd 10: (2 sc in next st, 1 sc in next 8 sts) 6 times. (60 sts)
Rnds 11–30: 1 sc in each st around. (20 Rnds of 60 sts)
Rnd 31: (2 sc in next st, 1 sc in next 9 sts) 6 times. (66 sts)
Rnd 32: 1 sc in each st around. (66 sts)
Rnd 33: (2 sc in next st, 1 sc in next 10 sts) 6 times.
(72 sts)
Rnd 34: 1 sc in each st around. (72 sts)
Rnd 35: (2 sc in next st, 1 sc in next 11 sts) 6 times. (78 sts)
Rnds 36–55: 1 sc in each st around. (20 Rnds of 78 sts)
Put the start of the current round at the back. Then fit the
face to the body by pushing the safety eyes through both
the face and the body, before fitting the washers on the
inside. As a guide, the top of the face, not including the
ruff, should be level with Rnd 10, which means the eyes
should be fixed between Rnds 19 and 20 of the body.
Stuff the body firmly and continue to stuff as you work
the next few rounds.
Rnd 56: (sc2tog, 1 sc in next 11 sts) 6 times. (72 sts)
Rnd 57: (sc2tog, 1 sc in next 10 sts) 6 times. (66 sts)
Rnd 58: (sc2tog, 1 sc in next 9 sts) 6 times. (60 sts)
Rnd 59: (sc2tog, 1 sc in next 8 sts) 6 times. (54 sts)
Rnd 60: (sc2tog, 1 sc in next 7 sts) 6 times. (48 sts)
Rnd 61: (sc2tog, 1 sc in next 6 sts) 6 times. (42 sts)
Rnd 62: (sc2tog, 1 sc in next 5 sts) 6 times. (36 sts)
Rnd 63: (sc2tog, 1 sc in next 4 sts) 6 times. (30 sts)
Rnd 64: (sc2tog, 1 sc in next 3 sts) 6 times. (24 sts)
Rnd 65: (sc2tog, 1 sc in next 2 sts) 6 times. (18 sts)
Rnd 66: (sc2tog, 1 sc in next st) 6 times. (12 sts)
Rnd 67: (sc2tog) 6 times. (6 sts)
Fasten off, leaving a length of yarn.
Finish stuffing firmly, then sew up the hole at the bottom.
Pull the yarn upward through the body to make the
bottom a bit more flat, then pass the yarn through the
body a couple of times before cutting it.
Sew the face to the body using the length of col 1 that
you left attached after making the ruff. As you sew it,
make sure you hide the tops of the loop stitches behind
the face.

LEGS (MAKE 2)
Using col 2, ch2.
Rnd 1: 6 sc in 2nd ch from hook. (6 sts)
Rnd 2: 2 sc in each st around. (12 sts)
Rnd 3: 2 sc in each st around. (24 sts)
Rnd 4: (2 sc in next st, 1 sc in next 3 sts) 6 times. (30 sts)
Rnd 5: (2 sc in next st, 1 sc in next 4 sts) 6 times. (36 sts)
Rnd 6: (2 sc in next st, 1 sc in next 5 sts) 6 times. (42 sts)
Rnd 7: (2 sc in next st, 1 sc in next 6 sts) 6 times. (48 sts)

Note: In the next round, you will make the toes using a
6dc-pop over two stitches. See page 159 for full details of
how to do this stitch.

Rnd 8: 1 sc in next 15 sts, (6dc-pop over next 2 sts, 1 sc in
next st) 6 times, 1 sc in next 15 sts. (42 sts)
Rnd 9–10: 1 sc in each st around. (2 Rnds of 42 sts)
Change to col 1.
Rnd 11: (sc2tog, 1 sc in next 5 sts) 6 times. (36 sts)
Rnd 12–15: 1 sc in each st around. (4 Rnds of 36 sts)
Rnd 16: (sc2tog, 1 sc in next 4 sts) 6 times. (30 sts)

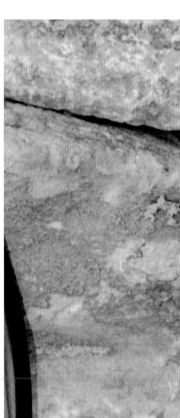
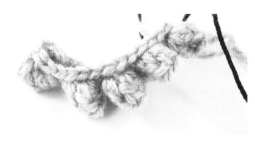

Rnd 17–20: 1 sc in each st around. (4 rnds of 30 sts)
Rnd 21: (sc2tog, 1 sc in next 3 sts) 6 times. (24 sts)
Rnd 22–25: 1 sc in each st around. (4 Rnds of 24 sts)
ss in next st and fasten off, leaving a long length of yarn. Stuff the legs, then sew them to the bottom of the body.

ARMS (MAKE 2)
To make fingers
You will make the fingers using a 6dc-pop over 2 ch. See page 159 for full details of how to achieve this stitch.
Using col 2, ch 17 loosely (if necessary use a larger hook just for the chain), 1 sc in 2nd ch from hook, (6dc-pop over next 2 ch, 1 sc in next ch) 5 times. (11 sts)
Rnd 1: (Place stitch marker before first sc) 1 sc into the back of next 16 ch, then work into the top of the popcorn stitches and sc as follows: 1 sc in next st, (1 sc in next st, 2 sc in next st) 5 times. (32 sts)
Rnds 2–3: 1 sc in each st around. (2 Rnds of 32 sts)

FOR LEFT ARM:
Rnd 4: 1 sc in next 15 sts, 6dc-pop over next 2 sts, 1 sc in next 15 sts. (31 sts)

FOR RIGHT ARM:
Rnd 4: 6dc-pop over next 2 sts, 1 sc in next 30 sts. (31 sts)

Change to col 1.
Rnd 5: 1 sc in each st around. (31 sts)
Rnd 6: sc2tog, 1 sc in next 29 sts. (30 sts)
Rnd 7: 1 sc in each st around. (30 sts)

Rnd 8: (sc2tog, 1 sc in next 8 sts) 3 times. (27 sts)
Rnds 9–10: 1 sc in each st around. (2 Rnds of 27 sts)
Rnd 11: (sc2tog, 1 sc in next 7 sts) 3 times. (24 sts)
Rnd 12–13: 1 sc in each st around. (2 Rnds of 24 sts)
Rnd 14: (sc2tog, 1 sc in next 6 sts) 3 times. (21 sts)
Rnd 15–19: 1 sc in each st around. (5 Rnds of 21 sts)
Rnd 20: (sc2tog, 1 sc in next 5 sts) 3 times. (18 sts)
Rnds 21–27: 1 sc in each st around. (7 Rnds of 18 sts)
Rnd 28: (sc2tog, 1 sc in next 4 sts) 3 times. (15 sts)
Rnd 29–35: 1 sc in each st around. (7 Rnds of 15 sts)
Stuff each arm, more firmly at the finger end, less toward the top.
Rnd 36: (sc2tog, 1 sc in next 3 sts) 3 times. (12 sts)
Rnd 37: (sc2tog, 1 sc in next 4 sts) twice. (10 sts)
ss into next st and fasten off, leaving a long length of yarn. Sew arms to either side of the body a little higher than the bottom of the face, about level with the top of Rnd 24 of the body.

Chubby baby

Chubby baby's big feet, button nose, adorable smile,
and comfy beanie hat make a fun and easily customized amigurumi!

NAME: **AMY KEMBER**
BIO: Amy is a technical writer living in Ottawa, Canada. Her interest in crochet began when she discovered an amigurumi book in a used bookstore. After making a pig, she was instantly hooked. Since 2010, Amy has been designing and selling her own amigurumi patterns on Etsy. www.etsy.com/shop/AmysGurumis/

DIFFICULTY:
★ ★ ☆ ☆ ☆

HOOK
F/5 (3.75mm)

YARN
In this project, we have used Bernat Handicrafter Cotton.
You will need to use DK weight yarn in your chosen colors.
Color 1: Skin (2 balls)
Color 2: Diaper (1 ball)
Color 3: Beanie (1 ball)

NOTIONS
1 pair 9mm safety eyes
Yarn needle
Fiberfill
Pink yarn

MEASUREMENTS
8½" (21.6cm) tall

APPROX TIME TAKEN
7 hours

CHUBBY BABY

HEAD
Using the hook and col 1, make a magic ring.
Rnd 1: 6 sc into ring and pull it closed. (6 sts)
Rnd 2: 2 sc in each sc (12 sts)
Rnd 3: (1 sc in next sc, 2 sc in the next sc) 6 times. (18 sts)
Rnd 4: (1 sc in each of next 2 sc, 2 sc in next sc) 6 times. (24 sts)
Rnd 5: (1 sc in each of next 3 sc, 2 sc in next sc) 6 times. (30 sts)
Rnd 6: (1 sc in each of next 4 sc, 2 sc in next sc) 6 times. (36 sts)
Rnd 7: (1 sc in each of next 5 sc, 2 sc in next sc) 6 times. (42 sts)
Rnd 8: (1 sc in each of next 6 sc, 2 sc in next sc) 6 times. (48 sts)
Rnds 9–16: 1 sc in each sc. (8 Rnds of 48 sts)
Rnd 17: (1 sc in each of next 6 sc, sc2tog in next 2 sc) 6 times. (42 sts)
Rnd 18: (1 sc in each of next 5 sc, sc2tog in next 2 sc) 6 times. (36 sts)
Rnd 19: (1 sc in each of next 4 sc, sc2tog in next 2 sc) 6 times. (30 sts)
Rnd 20: (1 sc in each of next 3 sc, sc2tog in next 2 sc) 6 times.(24 sts)
Rnd 21: (1 sc in each of next 2 sc, sc2tog in next 2 sc) 6 times. (18 sts)
Fasten off.

BODY
Using col 2, make a magic ring.
Rnd 1: 6 sc into ring and pull it closed. (6 sts)
Rnd 2: 2 sc in each sc. (12 sts)
Rnd 3: (1 sc in the next sc, 2 sc in the next sc) 6 times. (18 sts)
Rnd 4: (1 sc in each of next 2 sc, 2 sc in next sc) 6 times. (24 sts)
Rnd 5: (1 sc in each of next 3 sc, 2 sc in next sc) 6 times. (30 sts)
Rnd 6: (1 sc in each of next 4 sc, 2 sc in next sc) 6 times. (36 sts)
Rnds 7–10: 1 sc in each sc. (4 Rnds of 36 sts)
Change to col 1.
Rnd 11: 1 sc in back loops only in each sc. (36 sts)
Rnd 12: 1 sc in each sc. (36 sts)
Rnd 13: (1 sc in each of next 4 sc, sc2tog in next 2 sc) 6 times. (30 sts)
Rnd 14: 1 sc in each sc. (30 sts)
Rnd 15: (1 sc in each of next 3 sc, sc2tog in next 2 sc) 6 times. (24 sts)
Fasten off.

NOSE
Using col 1, make a magic ring.
Work 6 sc into ring and pull it closed. (6 sts)
Fasten off.

ARMS (MAKE 2)
Using col 1, make a magic ring.
Rnd 1: 6 sc into ring and pull it closed. (6 sts)
Rnd 2: 2 sc in each sc. (12 sts)

Rnds 3–8: 1 sc in each sc. (6 Rnds of 12 sts)
Rnd 9: (sc2tog in next 2 sc) 6 times. (6 sts)
Fasten off.

LEGS (MAKE 2)
Using col 1, make a magic ring.
Rnd 1: 6 sc into ring and pull it closed. (6 sts)
Rnd 2: 2 sc in each sc. (12 sts)
Rnd 3: (2 sc in each of next 3 sc, 1 sc in each of next 3 sc) twice. (18 sts)
Rnd 4: (1 sc in next sc, 2 sc in next sc) 3 times, 1 sc in each of next 3 sc, (1 sc in next sc, 2 sc in next sc) 3 times, 1 sc in each of next 3 sc. (24 sts)
Rnds 5–6: 1 sc in each sc. (2 Rnds of 24 sts)
Rnd 7: 1 dc in each of next 12 sc, 1 sc in each of next 12 sc. (24 sts)
Rnd 8: (sc2tog in next 2 dc) 6 times, 1 sc in each of next 12 sc. (18 sts)
Rnd 9: (1 sc in next sc, sc2tog in next 2 sc) 6 times. (12 sts)
Rnds 10–13: 1 sc in each sc. (4 Rnds of 12 sts)
Fasten off.

BEANIE
Using col 3, make a magic ring.
Rnd 1: 6 sc into ring and pull it closed. (6 sts)
Rnd 2: 2 sc in each sc. (12 sts)
Rnd 3: (1 sc in next sc, 2 sc in the next sc) 6 times. (18 sts)
Rnd 4: (1 sc in each of next 2 sc, 2 sc in next sc) 6 times. (24 sts)
Rnd 5: (1 sc in each of next 3 sc, 2 sc in next sc) 6 times. (30 sts)
Rnd 6: (1 sc in each of next 4 sc, 2 sc in next sc) 6 times. (36 sts)
Rnd 7: (1 sc in each of next 5 sc, 2 sc in next sc) 6 times. (42 sts)
Rnd 8: (1 sc in each of next 6 sc, 2 sc in next sc) 6 times. (48 sts)
Rnds 9–16: 1 sc in each sc. (8 Rnds of 48 sts)
Fasten off and weave in ends.

ASSEMBLE THE FACE
Insert the safety eyes between Rnd 12 and Rnd 13 of the head and position them three stitches apart. Sew the nose between the eyes using a yarn needle. Embroider a V-shaped mouth to the right of the nose on Rnd 16 using a yarn needle and pink yarn. Stuff the head firmly.

FINISHING

Stuff the body, arms, and legs.
Sew the body to the head—there is one extra decrease Rnd on the head than on the body so the last Rnd of the body (Rnd 15) should be sewn around the second to last Rnd on the head (Rnd 16).

Sew the arms to the body between Rnd 13 and Rnd 14, and position them nine stitches apart in the front.
Sew the legs to the body between Rnd 5 and Rnd 6, and position them one stitch apart in the front.

Trio of dinosaurs

Step back to the Jurassic era
with these adorable dinosaurs.

NAME:
MEVLINN GUSICK

BIO: Mevlinn is a college graduate with a BFA in Fine Arts Painting. Her interest in knitting and crochet began when her aunt suggested she try knitting. It piqued her curiosity and here she is today, crocheting amigurumi whenever she gets the chance, and giving them to those she loves.
www.mevvsan.com

DIFFICULTY:
★ ★ ☆ ☆ ☆

HOOK
C/2 (2.75mm)

YARN
In this project, we have used Rosario 4 Catitano. You will need medium weight yarn in your chosen colors.
Color 1: Body and tail (1 ball)
Color 2: Back spikes (scrap yarn)
Color 3: Tail spikes and toenails (scrap yarn)

NOTIONS
Fiberfill
1 pair 9mm safety eyes
Scissors
Yarn needle
Stitch marker (optional)

MEASUREMENTS
7 ¾" (19.7cm) head to tail

APPROX TIME TAKEN
6 hours

STEGOSAURUS

BODY
Using the hook and col 1, make a magic ring.
Rnd 1: 7 sc in magic ring. (7 sts)
Rnd 2: 2 sc in each st around. (14 sts)
Rnd 3: (2 sc in next st, 1 sc next st) 7 times. (21 sts)
Rnd 4: (2 sc in next st, 1 sc in next 2 sts) 7 times. (28 sts)
Rnd 5: (2 sc in next st, 1 sc in next 3 sts) 7 times. (35 sts)
Rnd 6: 1 sc in each st around. (35 sts)
Rnd 7: (2 sc in next st, 1 sc in next 4 sts) 7 times. (42 sts)
Rnd 8: 1 sc in each st around. (42 sts)
Rnd 9: 2 sc in next st, 1 sc in next 2 sts, 2 sc in next st, 1 sc in next 39 sts. (44 sts)

Note: Rnd 9 is the start of a side-specific increase made to create the "hump" of the Stegosaurus's back. Keep this in mind later when placing the eyes.

Rnd 10: 1 sc in each st around. (44 sts)
Rnd 11: 2 sc in next st, 1 sc in next st, 2 sc in next st, 1 sc in next 41 sts. (46 sts)
Rnds 12–13: 1 sc in each st around. (2 Rnds of 46 sts)
Rnd 14: sc2tog, 1 sc in next st, sc2tog, 1 sc in next 41 sts. (44 sts)
Rnd 15: 1 sc in each st around. (44 sts)
Rnd 16: sc2tog, 1 sc in next st, sc2tog, 1 sc in next 39 sts. (42 sts)
Rnd 17: 1 sc in each st around. (42 sts)
Rnd 18: (sc2tog, 1 sc in next 5 sts) 6 times. (36 sts)
Rnd 19: 1 sc in each st around. (36 sts)
Start stuffing and continue stuffing as you go.
Rnd 20: (sc2tog, 1 sc in next 4 sts) 6 times. (30 sts)
Rnd 21: 1 sc in each st around. (30 sts)
Rnd 22: (sc2tog, 1 sc in next 3 sts) 6 times. (24 sts)
Rnd 23: 1 sc in each st around. (24 sts)
Rnd 24: (sc2tog, 1 sc in next 2 sts) 6 times. (18 sts)
Rnds 25–27: 1 sc in each st around. (3 Rnds of 18 sts)
Fix the safety eyes between Rnds 25–27 with 8 sts between each eye.
Rnd 28: (sc2tog, 1 sc in next 7 sts) twice. (16 sts)
Rnd 29: (sc2tog, 1 sc in next 2 sts) 4 times. (12 sts)
Rnd 30: (sc2tog) 6 times. (6 sts)
Fasten off, leaving a tail for sewing. Using the yarn needle, weave the yarn tail through the front ring of each remaining st and pull it tight to close.

TAIL
Using col 1, make a magic ring.
Rnd 1: 4 sc in magic ring. (4 sts)
Rnd 2: 1 sc in each st around. (4 sts)
Rnd 3: 2 sc in next st, 1 sc in each remaining st to end. (5 sts)
Rnds 4–22: As Rnd 3. (24 sts after Rnd 22)

Fasten off, leaving a tail for sewing. Stuff the tail and sew it onto the body.

Note: When you sew the tail to the body, do so by placing the body on a table and pinning the tail in place first. You want the tail to be attached to the body but touching the table in a completely horizontal position. If you try and sew the tail at an angle to the body, you might find that the tail stops the legs from resting on the ground when you later sew them on.

FRONT LEGS (MAKE 2)
Using col 1, make a magic ring.
Rnd 1: 6 sc in magic ring. (6 sts)
Rnd 2: 2 sc in each st around. (12 sts)
Rnd 3 (blo): 1 sc in each st around. (12 sts)
Rnds 4–8: 1 sc in each st around. (5 Rnds of 12 sts)
Fasten off, leaving a long tail for sewing.

BACK LEGS (MAKE 2)
Using col 1, make a magic ring.
Rnds 1–8: As given for Front Legs. (12 sts)
Rnds 9–10: 1 sc in each st around. (2 Rnds of 12 sts)
Fasten off, leaving a long tail for sewing.

SEWING ON THE LEGS

First, stuff each leg firmly at the bottom, and less firmly at the top so that you can pinch the opening shut, folding it in half. Now find a spot on the side of the dinosaur where you want to attach the leg. Hold the body while you're doing this and position it above a table. You want the legs to give the body enough lift off the table so that the stomach won't touch the table.

Thread your yarn and sew only the top half of the leg in place. Then sew one Row down and continue sewing the rest of the leg in place. It should be very thin at the joint and may be awkward. Instead of fastening off, thread the yarn to the underside of the leg and begin sewing the leg to the body, one st at a time. Go down the leg about 3–5 sts until you see the bowed leg finally tighten up and line up straight with the side of the body. When you are happy with the leg, fasten off, and weave the yarn end into the body.

Note: The stegosaurus has longer hind legs than front, so allow for this when attaching them. Always keep in mind how you want your dinosaur's finished position to be when attaching their legs.

SMALL SPIKE (MAKE 6)

Using col 2, make a magic ring.
Rnd 1: 5 sc in magic ring. (5 sts)
Rnd 2: 2 sc in each st around. (10 sts)
Rnd 3: (sc2tog) 5 times. (5 sts)
Fasten off, leaving a long tail for sewing. Do not stuff the spikes.

MEDIUM SPIKE (MAKE 4)

Using col 2, make a magic ring.
Rnd 1: 5 sc in magic ring. (5 sts)
Rnd 2: 2 sc in each st around. (10 sts)
Rnd 3: (2 sc in next st, 1 sc in next 4 sts) twice. (12 sts)
Rnd 4: (sc2tog, 1 sc in next 4 sts) twice. (10 sts)
Rnd 5: (sc2tog) 5 times. (5 sts)
Fasten off, leaving a long tail for sewing. Do not stuff the spikes.

LARGE SPIKE (MAKE 2)

Using col 2, make a magic ring.
Rnd 1: 5 sc in magic ring. (5 sts)
Rnd 2: 2 sc in each st around. (10 sts)
Rnd 3: (2 sc in next st, 1 sc in next st) 5 times. (15 sts)
Rnd 4: 1 sc in each st around. (15 sts)
Rnd 5: (sc2tog, 1 sc in next st) 5 times. (10 sts)
Rnd 6: (sc2tog) 5 times. (5 sts)
Fasten off, leaving a long tail for sewing.
Do not stuff the spikes.

FINISHING

Sew the spikes evenly spaced down the body and tail of the stegosaurus. Starting at the head, you will have two rows of spikes side by side in the following order, working from front to back: Small/Medium/Large/Medium/Small/Small.
The two rows maintain a little over a finger's width apart but narrow more as they reach the tail and head.

TOENAILS

Using col 3, cut a length of yarn about as long as your arm, and attach it to the edge of the foot, ch 3, 1 sc back into the same st (one toenail made). *Pull the yarn through as if you were fastening off, but instead thread a needle and move the yarn two sts to the left for the next toenail, ch 3, 1 sc back into the same st; rep from * once more to make the third and final toenail. Fasten off, then weave in all yarn ends.

TAIL SPIKES (MAKE 4)

Using col 3, make a magic ring.
Rnd 1: 4 sc in magic ring. (4 sts)
Rnd 2: 2 sc in next st, 1 sc in each remaining st. (5 sts)
Rnd 3: 1 sc in each st around. (5 sts)
Rnd 4: 2 sc in next st, 1 sc in each remaining st. (6 sts)
Rnd 5: 1 sc in each st around. (6 sts)
Fasten off, leaving a long tail for sewing. Do not stuff the spikes. Sew the spikes to the tip of the dinosaur's tail, two on each side.

Did you know?

It is believed that the earliest forms of crochet were created using a bent finger instead of a hook.

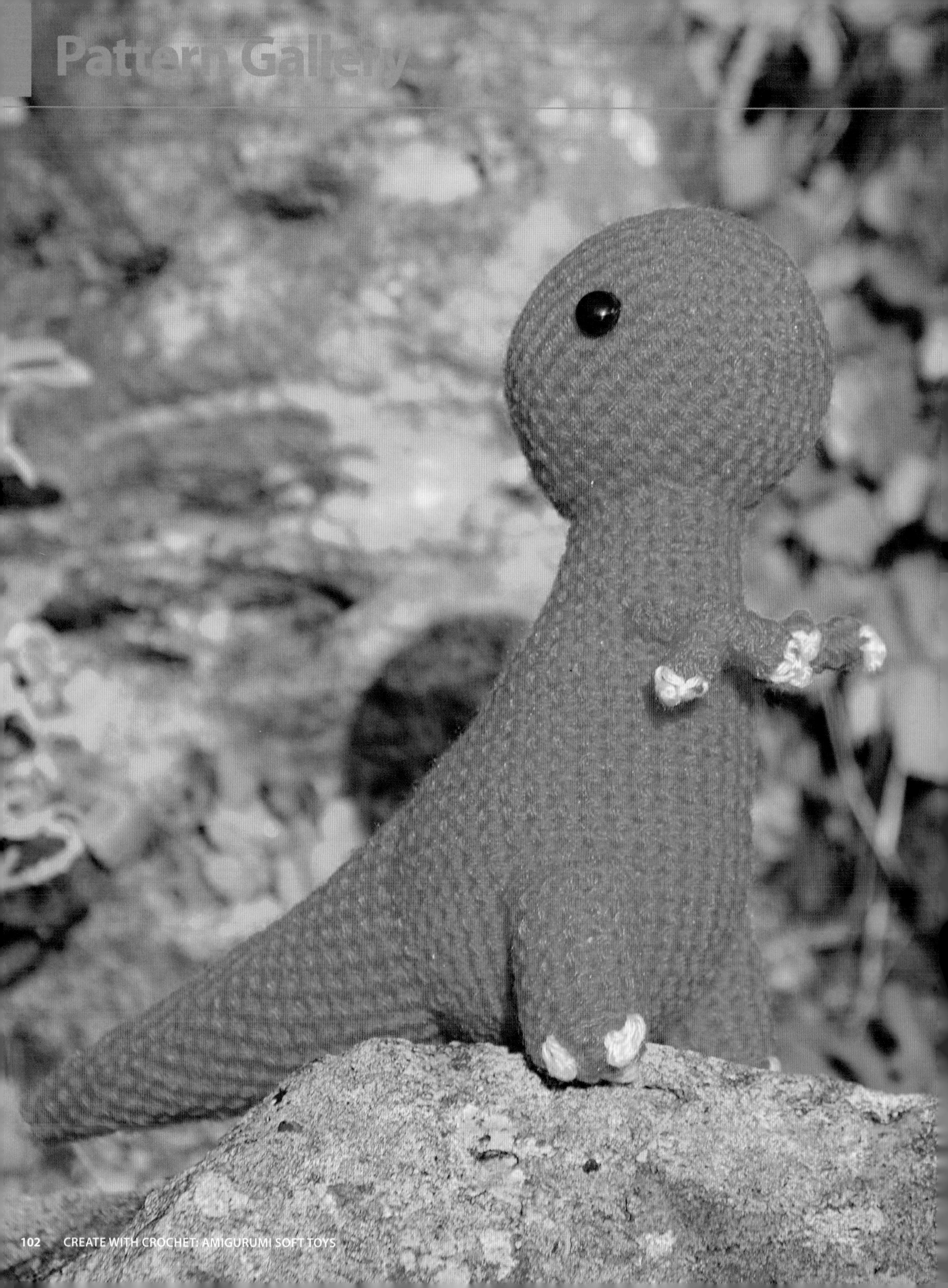

DIFFICULTY:
★ ★ ★ ☆ ☆

HOOK
C/2 (2.75mm)

YARN
In this project, we have used
Rosario 4 Catitano. You will need
medium yarn in your choice of
colors.
Color 1: Body (1 ball)
Color 2: Toenails and claws (scrap
yarn)

NOTIONS
Fiberfill
1 pair 12mm safety eyes
Scissors
Yarn needle
Stitch marker (optional)

MEASUREMENTS
9 ¾" (24.8cm) head to tail

APPROX TIME TAKEN
6 hours

T-REX

BODY

Using the hook and col 1, make a magic ring.
Rnd 1: 6 sc in magic ring. (6 sts)
Rnd 2: 2 sc in each st around. (12 sts)
Rnd 3: (2 sc in next st, 1 sc in next st) 6 times. (18 sts)
Rnd 4: (2 sc in next st, 1 sc in next 2 sts) 6 times. (24 sts)
Rnd 5: (2 sc in next st, 1 sc in next 3 sts) 6 times. (30 sts)
Rnd 6: (2 sc in next st, 1 sc in next 4 sts) 6 times. (36 sts)
Rnd 7: 1 sc in each st around. (36 sts)
Rnd 8: (2 sc in next st, 1 sc in next 5 sts) 6 times. (42 sts)
Rnds 9–10: 1 sc in each st around. (2 Rnds of 42 sts)
Rnd 11: sc2tog, 1 sc in each remaining st to end. (41 sts)
Rnds 12–14: As Rnd 11. (38 sts after Rnd 14)
Stuff with fiberfill and continue stuffing as you go.
Rnd 15: sc2tog, 1 sc in next 33 sts, sc2tog, 1 sc in last st. (36 sts)
Rnd 16: sc2tog, 1 sc in next 31 sts, sc2tog, 1 sc in last st. (34 sts)
Rnd 17: sc2tog, 1 sc in next 29 sts, sc2tog, 1 sc in last st. (32 sts)
Rnd 18: sc2tog, 1 sc in next 27 sts, sc2tog, 1 sc in last st. (30 sts)
Rnd 19: sc2tog, 1 sc in next 25 sts, sc2tog, 1 sc in last st. (28 sts)
Rnd 20: sc2tog, 1 sc in next 23 sts, sc2tog, 1 sc in last st. (26 sts)
Rnd 21: sc2tog, 1 sc in each remaining st to end. (25 sts)
Rnds 22–26: As Rnd 21. (20 sts after Rnd 26)
Fasten off, leaving a long tail for sewing.

HEAD

Using col 1, make a magic ring.
Rnd 1: 6 sc in magic ring. (6 sts)
Rnd 2: 2 sc in each st around. (12 sts)
Rnd 3: (2 sc in next st, 1 sc in next st) 6 times. (18 sts)
Rnd 4: (2 sc in next st, 1 sc in next 2 sts) 6 times. (24 sts)
Rnd 5: (2 sc in next st, 1 sc in next 3 sts) 6 times. (30 sts)
Rnd 6: (2 sc in next st, 1 sc in next 4 sts) 6 times. (36 sts)
Rnds 7–15: 1 sc in each st around. (9 Rnds of 36 sts)
Rnd 16: (sc2tog, 1 sc in next 4 sts) 6 times. (30 sts)
Rnd 17: (sc2tog, 1 sc in next 3 sts) 6 times. (24 sts)
Fix the safety eyes 11 rows down from the magic ring with 13 sts between each eye.
Start stuffing and continue stuffing as you go.
Rnd 18: (sc2tog, 1 sc in next 2 sts) 6 times. (18 sts)
Rnd 19: (sc2tog, 1 sc in next st) 6 times. (12 sts)
Rnd 20: (sc2tog) 6 times. (6 sts)

Fasten off, leaving a tail for sewing. Using the yarn needle, weave the yarn tail through the front ring of each remaining st and pull it tight to close. Using the tail end of yarn from the body, sew the head to the body. (The back of the neck should be sewn onto the head approx 6 Rnds away from the head's magic ring.)

TAIL

Using col 1, make a magic ring.
Rnd 1: 4 sc in magic ring. (4 sts)
Rnd 2: 1 sc in each st around. (4 sts)
Rnd 3: 2 sc in next st, 1 sc in each remaining st. (5 sts)

Rnds 4–25: As Rnd 2. (27 sts after Rnd 25)

Fasten off, leaving a long tail for sewing. Stuff the tail with fiberfill and sew it to the body as follows:
Place the body on a table in an upright position and pin the tail in place first. If you try to sew the tail on at an angle to the body, you might find that it stops the legs from resting on the ground when you sew them on later.

LEGS (MAKE 2)

Using col 1, make a magic ring.
Rnd 1: 6 sc in magic ring (6 sts)
Rnd 2: 2 sc in each st around. (12 sts)
Rnd 3 (blo): 1 sc in each st around. (12 sts)
Rnds 4–9: 1 sc in each st around. (6 Rnds of 12 sts)
Fasten off, leaving a long tail for sewing.

ARMS (MAKE 2)

Using col 1, make a magic ring.
Rnd 1: 4 sc in magic ring. (4 sts)
Rnds 2–7: 1 sc in each st around. (6 Rnds of 4 sts)
Fasten off, leaving a long tail for sewing.

FINGERS (MAKE 2)

Using col 1, make a magic ring.
Rnd 1: 4 sc in magic ring. (4 sts)
Rnds 2–3: 1 sc in each st around. (2 Rnds of 4 sts)
Fasten off, leaving a long tail for sewing.
When both the arms and fingers are complete, sew the finger to the arm, so that the end of the arm and the finger are both of equal length. Sew the arms to the body approximately seven to eight rows below the point where the head attaches to the body.

TOENAILS

Using col 2, cut a length of yarn about as long as your arm, and attach it to the edge of the foot, ch 3, 1 sc back into the same st (one toenail made). *Pull the yarn through two sts to the left for the next toenail, ch 3, 1 sc back into the same st; rep from * once more to make the final toenail. Fasten off, weave in all yarn ends.

CLAWS

Using col 2, cut a short piece of yarn, pull the yarn through a st at the tip of a finger, ch 1, move the hook to a st to the left of the finger, 1 sc, ch 1, pull the yarn through, and then fasten off. Weave in the yarn ends gently to avoid distorting the ch 1 tip of the claw you just made.

FINISHING

First, stuff each leg firmly at the bottom, and less firmly at the top so that you can pinch the opening shut, folding it in half. Now, find a spot on the side of the dinosaur where you want to attach the leg. Hold the body above a table as far as you want it to stand when all the legs are sewn on. Go down the leg about 3–5 sts until you see the bowed leg finally tighten and line up straight with the side of the body. Fasten off and weave in the yarn end.

Note: To keep all legs even you need to attach each leg at the exact same Row on the body.

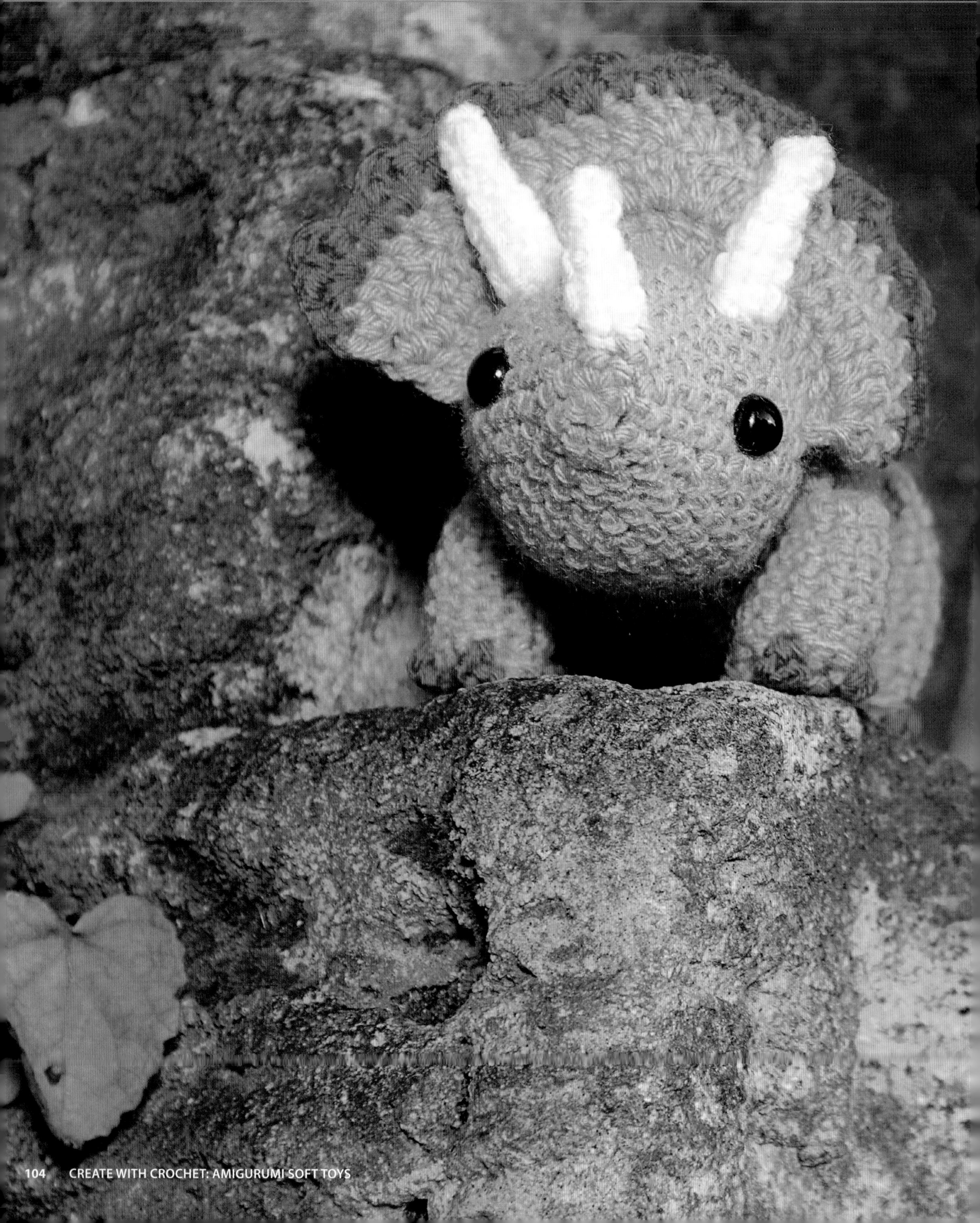

TRICERATOPS

BODY
Using the hook and col 1, make a magic ring.
Rnd 1: 7 sc in magic ring. (7 sts)
Rnd 2: 2 sc in each st around. (14 sts)
Rnd 3: (2 sc in next st, 1 sc next st) 7 times. (21 sts)
Rnd 4: (2 sc in next st, 1 sc in next 2 sts) 7 times. (28 sts)
Rnd 5: (2 sc in next st, 1 sc in next 3 sts) 7 times. (35 sts)
Rnd 6: 1 sc in each st around. (35 sts)
Rnd 7: (2 sc in next st, 1 sc in next 4 sts) 7 times. (42 sts)
Rnds 8–13: 1 sc in each st around. (6 Rnds of 42 sts)
Rnd 14: (sc2tog, 1 sc in next 5 sts) 6 times. (36 sts)
Rnd 15: 1 sc in each st around. (36 sts)
Fill with fiberfill and continue stuffing as you go.
Rnd 16: (sc2tog, 1 sc in next 7 sts) 4 times. (32 sts)
Rnd 17: 1 sc in each st around. (32 sts)
Rnd 18: (sc2tog, 1 sc in next 6 sts) 4 times. (28 sts)
Rnds 19–20: 1 sc in each st around. (2 Rnds of 28 sts)
Fasten off, leaving a tail for sewing.

HEAD
Using col 1, make a magic ring.
Rnd 1: 6 sc in magic ring. (6 sts)
Rnd 2: 2 sc in each st around. (12 sts)
Rnd 3: 1 sc in each st around. (12 sts)
Rnd 4: (2 sc in next st, 1 sc in next st) 6 times. (18 sts)
Rnd 5: 1 sc in each st around. (18 sts)
Rnd 6: (2 sc in next st, 1 sc in next 2 sts) 6 times. (24 sts)
Rnd 7: (2 sc in next st, 1 sc in next 3 sts) 6 times. (30 sts)
Rnd 8: (2 sc in next st, 1 sc in next 4 sts) 6 times. (36 sts)
Rnds 9–11: 1 sc in each st around. (3 Rnds of 36 sts)
Rnd 12: 1 scblo in next 18 sts (this will help you to identify where to crochet the head crest later), 1 sc in each remaining st (working through both rings). (36 sts)
Rnd 13: (sc2tog, 1 sc in next 4 sts) 6 times. (30 sts)
Fix the safety eyes seven rows down from magic ring with 14 sts between each eye.
Start stuffing and continue stuffing as you go.

Rnd 14: (sc2tog, 1 sc in next 3 sts) 6 times. (24 sts)
Rnd 15: (sc2tog, 1 sc in next 2 sts) 6 times. (18 sts)
Rnd 16: (sc2tog, 1 sc in next st) 6 times. (12 sts)
Rnd 17: (sc2tog) 6 times. (6 sts)
Fasten off, leaving a tail for sewing.
Weave the yarn tail through the front ring of each remaining st and pull it tight to close.

HEAD CREST
Using col 1, with the front of the triceratops's head facing you, attach the yarn with a sl st to the far right unworked ring from Rnd 12 of the head.
Row 1: ch 3 (counts as 1 dc), dc in the same ring at base of ch 3, 1 dc in next 7 rings, 2 dc in next 2 rings, 1 dc in next 7 rings, 2 dc in last ring, turn. (22 sts)
Row 2: ch 2, (counts as 1 hdc), 1 hdc in same st at base of ch 2, 1 dc in next 9 sts, 2 dc in next 2 sts, 1 dc in next 9 sts, 2 hdc in last st, turn. (26 sts)
Row 3: ch 2, 1 hdc in same st at base of ch 2, 1 dc in next 11 sts, 2 dc in next 2 sts, 1 dc in next 11 sts, 2 hdc in last st, turn. (30 sts)
Change to col 2.
Row 4: *1 sc in next 2 sts, (1 hdc, ch 2, 1 hdc) in next st; rep from * to end.
Fasten off, weave in ends.

HEAD HORNS (MAKE 2)
Using col 3, make a magic ring.
Rnd 1: 4 sc in magic ring. (4 sts)
Rnd 2: 1 sc in each st around. (4 sts)
Rnd 3: 2 sc in next st, 1 sc in next 3 sts. (5 sts)
Rnd 4: 2 sc in next st, 1 sc in next 4 sts. (6 sts)
Rnd 5: 2 sc in next st, 1 sc in next 5 sts. (7 sts)
Rnd 6: 2 sc in next st, 1 sc in next 6 sts. (8 sts)
Fasten off, leaving a tail for sewing. Lightly fill with fiberfill, if needed, and sew each horn above each eye.

NOSE HORN
Using col 3, make a magic ring.
Rnd 1: 4 sc in magic ring. (4 sts)
Rnd 2: 1 sc in each st around. (4 sts)
Rnd 3: 2 sc in next st, 1 sc in next 3 sts. (5 sts)
Rnd 4: 2 sc in next st, 1 sc in next 4 sts. (6 sts)
Rnd 5: 2 sc in next st, 1 sc in next 5 sts. (7 sts)
Fasten off, leaving a tail for sewing. Lightly stuff with fiberfill, if needed, and sew this horn to the tip of the nose.

Using the tail end of yarn from the body, sew the head to the body.

TAIL
Using col 1, make a magic ring.
Rnd 1: 4 sc in magic ring. (4 sts)
Rnd 2: 1 sc in each st around. (4 sts)
Rnd 3: 2 sc in next st, 1 sc in each remaining st to end. (5 sts)
Rnds 4–21: As Rnd 3. (23 sts after Rnd 21)
Fasten off, leaving a long tail for sewing. Stuff the tail with fiberfill and sew it onto the body as follows:

DIFFICULTY:
★ ★ ★ ☆ ☆

HOOK
C/2 (2.75mm)

YARN
In this project, we have used Rosario 4 Catitano. You will need medium weight yarn in your chosen colors.
Color 1: Body (1 ball)
Color 2: Crest and toenails (scrap yarn)
Color 3: Horns (scrap yarn)

NOTIONS
Fiberfill
1 pair 12mm safety eyes
Scissors
Yarn needle
Stitch marker (optional)

MEASUREMENTS
9 ¾" (24.8cm) head to tail

APPROX TIME TAKEN
6 hours

Place the body onto a table and pin the tail in place first. You want the tail to be attached to the body and be completely horizontal with the table. If you try to sew the tail on at an angle to the body, you might find that the tail stops the legs from resting on the ground when you later sew them on.

FRONT LEGS (MAKE 2)
Using col 1, make a magic ring.
Rnd 1: 6 sc in magic ring. (6 sts)
Rnd 2: 2 sc in each st around. (12 sts)
Rnd 3 (blo): 1 sc in each st around. (12 sts)
Rnds 4–9: 1 sc in each st around. (6 Rnds of 12 sts)
Fasten off, leaving a long tail for sewing.

BACK LEGS (MAKE 2)
Using col 1, make a magic ring.
Rnds 1–9: As given for Front Legs. (12 sts)
Rnd 10: 1 sc in each st around. (12 sts)
Fasten off, leaving a long tail for sewing.

SEWING ON THE LEGS
Hold the body while you're doing this, and position it above a table as far as you want it to stand when all the legs are sewn on. You want the legs to give the body enough lift off the table so that the stomach won't touch the table when it is completely assembled.
First, stuff each leg firmly at the bottom, and less firmly at the top so that you can pinch the opening shut, folding it

in half. Now, find a spot on the side of the dinosaur where you want to attach the leg.
Thread your yarn and sew only the top half of the leg in place. Then sew one Row down and continue sewing the rest of the leg in place into this row. It should be very thin at the joint and may be awkward. Instead of fastening off, thread the yarn to the underside of the leg and begin sewing the leg to the body, one st at a time. Go down the leg about 3–5 sts until you see the bowed leg finally tighten and line up straight with the side of the body. When you are happy with the leg, fasten off and weave the yarn end into the body.

Note: The triceratops has longer hind legs, and this helps to push its face closer to the ground, so make sure you attach the legs to different rows to make it even. Always keep in mind how you want your dinosaur's finished position to be when attaching their legs.

TOENAILS
Using col 2, cut a length of yarn about as long as your arm, and attach it to the edge of the foot, ch 4, 1 dc back into the same st (one toenail made). *Pull the yarn through as if you were fastening off, but instead thread a needle and move the yarn two sts to the left for the next toenail, ch 4, 1 dc back into the same st; rep from * once more to make the third and final toenail. Fasten off, weave in all yarn ends.

Little bunny

Use up leftover yarn to crochet a little bunny with fun, striped legs
and a cute removable T-shirt!

NAME: **AMY KEMBER**
BIO: Amy is a technical writer living in Ottawa, Canada. Her interest in crochet began when she discovered an amigurumi book in a used bookstore. After making a pig, she was instantly hooked. Since 2010, Amy has been designing and selling her own amigurumi patterns on Etsy.
www.etsy.com/shop/
AmysGurumis/

DIFFICULTY:
★ ★ ★ ☆ ☆

HOOK
F/5 (3.75mm)

YARN
In this project, we have used Bernat Handicrafter Cotton. You will need to use DK weight yarn in your chosen colors.
Color 1: Skin (1 ball)
Color 2: Dark stripe (1 ball)
Color 3: Light stripe (1 ball)
Color 4: Shirt (1 ball)

NOTIONS
1 pair 9mm safety eyes
Yarn needle
Fiberfill
Pink and white felt
Hot glue gun
Small pom-pom for tail

MEASUREMENTS
9¾" (24.8cm) tall

APPROX TIME TAKEN
8 hours

LITTLE BUNNY

HEAD
Using the hook and col 1, make a magic ring.
Rnd 1: 6 sc into ring and pull it closed. (6 sts)
Rnd 2: 2 sc in each sc. (12 sts)
Rnd 3: (1 sc in next sc, 2 sc in the next sc) 6 times. (18 sts)
Rnd 4: (1 sc in each of next 2 sc, 2 sc in next sc) 6 times. (24 sts)
Rnd 5: (1 sc in each of next 3 sc, 2 sc in next sc) 6 times. (30 sts)
Rnd 6: (1 sc in each of next 4 sc, 2 sc in next sc) 6 times. (36 sts)
Rnds 7–13: 1 sc in each sc. (7 Rnds of 36 sts)
Rnd 14: (1 sc in each of next 4 sc, sc2tog in next 2 sc) 6 times. (30 sts)
Rnd 15: (1 sc in each of next 3 sc, sc2tog in next 2 sc) 6 times. (24 sts)
Rnd 16: (1 sc in each of next 2 sc, sc2tog in next 2 sc) 6 times. (18 sts)
Rnd 17: (1 sc in next sc, sc2tog in next 2 sc) 6 times. (12 sts)
Fasten off.

BODY
Using col 2, make a magic ring.
Rnd 1: 6 sc into ring and pull it closed. (6 sts)
Rnd 2: 2 sc in each sc. (12 sts)
Rnd 3: (1 sc in next sc, 2 sc in next sc) 6 times. (18 sts)
Change to col 3.
Rnd 4: (1 sc in each of next 2 sc, 2 sc in next sc) 6 times. (24 sts)
Rnd 5: (1 sc in each of next 3 sc, 2 sc in next sc) 6 times. (30 sts)
Change to col 2.
Rnds 6–7: 1 sc in each sc. (2 Rnds of 30 sts)
Change to col 3.
Rnds 8–9: 1 sc in each sc. (2 Rnds of 30 sts)
Change to col 1.
Rnds 10–11: 1 sc in each sc. (2 Rnds of 30 sts)
Rnd 12: (1 sc in each of next 3 sc, sc2tog in next 2 sc) 6 times. (24 sts)
Rnds 13–15: 1 sc in each sc. (3 Rnds of 24 sts)
Rnd 16: (1 sc in each of next 2 sc, sc2tog in next 2 sc) 6 times. (18 sts)
Fasten off.

EARS (MAKE 2)
Using col 1, make a magic ring.
Rnd 1: 6 sc into ring and pull it closed.
Rnd 2: 2 sc in each sc. (12 sts)
Rnd 3: (1 sc in next sc, 2 sc in next sc) 6 times. (18 sts)
Rnd 4: (1 sc in each of next 2 sc, 2 sc in next sc) 6 times. (24 sts)
Rnd 5: (1 sc in each of next 3 sc, 2 sc in next sc) 6 times. (30 sts)
Rnd 6: 1 sc in each sc. (30 sts)
Fasten off.

ARMS (MAKE 2)
Using col 1, make a magic ring.
Rnd 1: 4 sc into ring and pull it closed.
Rnd 2: 2 sc in each sc. (8 sts)
Rnds 3–10: 1 sc in each sc. (8 Rnds of 8 sts)
Fasten off.

LEGS (MAKE 2)
Using col 2, make a magic ring.
Rnd 1: 5 sc into ring and pull it closed. (5 sts)
Rnd 2: 2 sc in each sc. (10 sts)
Change to col 3.
Rnds 3–4: 1 sc in each sc. (2 Rnds of 10 sts)
Change to col 2.
Rnds 5–6: 1 sc in each sc. (2 Rnds of 10 sts)
Change to col 3.
Rnds 7–8: 1 sc in each sc. (2 Rnds of 10 sts)
Change to col 2.
Rnds 9–10: 1 sc in each sc. (2 Rnds of 10 sts)
Change to col 3.
Rnds 11–12: 1 sc in each sc. (2 Rnds of 10 sts)
Fasten off.

SHIRT
Using col 4, ch 25, join in 1st ch with ss.
Rnd 1: (1 sc in each of next 4 sc, 2 sc in next sc) 5 times. (30 sts)
Rnd 2: (1 sc in each of next 5 sc, 2 sc in next sc) 5 times. (35 sts)
Rnd 3: (1 sc in each of next 6 sc, 2 sc in next sc) 5 times. (40 sts)
Rnd 4 (make sleeves): skip 11 sc, join in 12th sc with ss, 2 sc in each of next 8 sc, skip 11 sc, join in 32nd sc with ss, 2 sc in each of next 8 sc. (32 sts—do not count the slip sts from this Rnd as sts in the following rnd)
Rnds 5–9: 1 sc in each sc. (5 Rnds of 32 sts)
Fasten off.

ASSEMBLE THE FACE
Insert the safety eyes between Rnd 12 and Rnd 13 of the head, and position them 6 sts apart.
Stuff the head firmly.
Cut out a pink felt nose and a cream felt muzzle using shapes of your choice.
Glue the nose to the muzzle using a hot glue gun.
Position the muzzle and nose between the eyes but slightly higher up on the face between Rnd 8 and Rnd 12.
Glue the muzzle and nose to the face with a hot glue gun. If you don't have a hot glue gun, you can embroider the nose and muzzle together, and then embroider the face on with the yarn or thread of your choice.

FINISHING

Stuff the body, arms, and legs. Sew the body to the head.

NOTE: There is one extra decrease Rnd on the head than on the body, so the last Rnd of the body should be sewn around the second to last Rnd on the head.
Sew the arms to the body between Rnd 13 and Rnd 15, and position them 6 sts apart in the front.
Sew the legs to the body between Rnd 4 and Rnd 5, and position them 2 sts apart in the front.
Sew the ears to the head between Rnd 2 and Rnd 4.

Pearl the dolphin

Requiring only basic stitches and a small amount of yarn,
Pearl is a quick and cute amigurumi that can take shape in just an afternoon!

NAME: SARAH SLOYER
BIO: When Sarah first discovered amigurumi, she became determined to teach herself how to crochet so she could make them! After lots of practice, she is finally designing and writing her own patterns, which she loves sharing with others.
www.ravelry.com/stores/critterbeans

DIFFICULTY:
★ ★ ★ ☆ ☆

HOOK
D/3 (3.25mm)

YARN
In this project, we used Lion Brand Vanna's Choice. You will need medium weight yarn in your chosen colors.
Color 1: Body (1 ball)
Color 2: Belly (1 ball)

NOTIONS
1 pair 9mm safety eyes
Fiberfill
Scissors
Stitch markers
Yarn needle

MEASUREMENTS
4½" (11.4cm) long, 3" (7.6cm) tall

APPROX TIME TAKEN
4 hours

PEARL THE DOLPHIN

BODY
Using the hook and col 1, ch 8.
Rnd 1: 1 sc in 2nd ch from hook, 1 sc in next 5 ch, 4 sc in next ch, rotate and work along the opposite side of foundation chain, 1 sc in next 5ch, 4 sc in next ch. You will now have a small oval shape. Place stitch marker in next st (this is be the first st of next round). (19 sts)
Rnd 2: 1 sc in next 7 sts, 3 sc in next st, 2 sc in next st, 1 sc in next 7 sts, 3 sc in next st, 2 sc in next st, 1 sc in next st. (25 sts)
Rnd 3: 1 sc in next 8 sts, 2 sc in next 3 sts, 1 sc in next 10 sts, 2 sc in next 3 sts, 1 sc in next st. (31 sts)
Rnd 4: 1 sc in next 7 sts, (2 sc in next st, 1 sc in next st) 5 times, 1 sc in next 9 sts, 2 sc in next 3 sts, 1 sc in next 2 sts. (39 sts)
Rnd 5: 1 sc in each st around. (39 sts)
Rnd 6: 1 sc in next 33 sts, 2 sc in next 3 sts, 1 sc in next 3 sts. (42 sts)
Rnd 7: 1 sc in each st around. (42 sts)
Rnd 8: 1 sc in next 10 sts, (2 sc in next st, 1 sc in next 2 sts) 4 times, 1 sc in next 13 sts, 2 sc in next 3 sts, 1 sc in next 4 sts. (49 sts)
Rnd 9: 1 sc in each st around. (49 sts)
Rnd 10: 1 sc in next 40 sts, 2 sc in next 3 sts, 1 sc in next 6 sts. (52 sts)
Rnd 11: 1 sc in next 15 sts, 2 sc in next 5 sts, 1 sc in next 32 sts. (57 sts)

Note: On Rnds 11 and 12, the stitches that form the dolphin's nose are very tight because of the multiple increases packed closely together from the previous rounds. It may be hard to see and work into these stitches; take your time so that you don't miss any.

Rnd 12: 1 sc in next 18 sts, 2 sc in next 4 sts, 1 sc in next 25 sts, 2 sc in next 3 sts, 1 sc in next 7 sts. (64 sts)
Rnd 13: 1 sc in each st around. (64 sts)

Note: Rnds 13, 14, and 15 are all shaped using lots of unevenly spaced decreases. Keep track of your stitches as you go by crossing stitches off.

Rnd 14: 1 sc in next st, sc2tog, 1 sc in next 5 sts, sc2tog, 1 sc in next 7 sts, (sc2tog) 5 times, 1 sc in next 7 sts, sc2tog, 1 sc in next 6 sts, sc2tog, 1 sc in next 8 sts, sc2tog, 1 sc in next st, sc2tog, 1 sc in next 6 sts, 1 sc in last st changing to col 2. (53 sts)

Rnd 15: 1 sc in next st, sc2tog, 1 sc in next 3 sts, sc2tog, 1 sc in next 4 sts, (sc2tog) 4 times, 1 sc in next 4 sts, sc2tog, 1 sc in next 5 sts, sc2tog, 1 sc in next 8 sts, (sc2tog) twice, 1 sc in next 6 sts. (43 sts)
Rnd 16: sc2tog, 1 sc in next 5 sts, sc2tog, 1 sc in next 4 sts, sc2tog, 1 sc in next 4 sts, sc2tog, 1 sc in next 5 sts, sc2tog, 1 sc in next 5 sts, sc2tog, 1 sc in next st, sc2tog, 1 sc in next 5 sts. (36 sts)
Rnd 17: 1 sc in next 2 sts, sc2tog, (1 sc in next 4 sts, sc2tog) 5 times, 1 sc in next 2 sts. (30 sts)

Next, fix the eyes as follows: count three rounds up from where col 2 starts. Starting at the tip of the nose, count 10 stitches away on either side and place each eye (18 stitches between them).

Rnd 18: (1 sc in next 3 sts, sc2tog) 6 times. (24 sts)
Rnd 19: 1 sc in next st, sc2tog, (1 sc in next 2 sts, sc2tog) 5 times, 1 sc in next st. (18 sts)

Begin stuffing the body firmly. Poke the stuffing into the nose to fill in its shape, and toward the sides of the dolphin's body, until the decreases made in the previous rounds are less prominent and the body is rounder.

Rnd 20: (1 sc in next st, sc2tog) 6 times. (12 sts)
Continue stuffing the body as you complete the final rounds. You can use the blunt end of your hook to push the stuffing up into the body.
Rnd 21: (sc2tog) 6 times. (6 sts)

Cut the yarn and fasten off, leaving a long tail. Thread the yarn tail through the front rings of the remaining 6 sts, then pull tight to gather.

TAIL FINS (MAKE 2)

In col 1, make a magic ring.
Rnd 1 (RS): 6 sc in magic ring. (6 sts)
Rnd 2: (1 sc in next 2 sts, 2 sc in next st) twice. (8 sts)
Rnd 3: 1 sc in each st around. (8 sts)
Rnd 4: (1 sc in next 3 sts, 2 sc in next st) twice. (10 sts)
Rnd 5: 1 sc in each st around. (10 sts)

When you have completed the first fin, fasten off. When you have completed the second fin, do not fasten off.
Join the two fins together as follows: with your working yarn (and second fin) still on your hook, insert the hook into the first stitch of the first fin. Yarn over and pull through a slip stitch. Ch 1, sc around both fins, creating one piece. When you have single crocheted around once, fasten off with a slip stitch. Do not stuff; press flat and set aside for assembly.

DORSAL FIN

In col 1, make a magic ring.
Rnd 1 (RS): 6 sc in magic ring. (6 sts).
Rnd 2: 1 sc in each st around. (6 sts)
Rnd 3: 2 sc in next 3 sts, 1 sc in next 3 sts. (9 sts)
Rnd 4: 1 sc in each st around. (9 sts)
Rnd 5: 1 sc in next 2 sts, 2 sc in next 2 st, 1 sc in next 5 sts. (11 sts)
Fasten off and leave a long tail for sewing. Do not stuff; press flat and set aside for assembly.

SIDE FINS (MAKE 2)

In col 1, make a magic ring.
Rnd 1 (RS): 6 sc in magic ring. (6 sts).
Rnd 2: 1 sc in each st around. (6 sts)
Rnd 3: (1 sc in next st, 2 sc in next st) 3 times. (9 sts)
Rnd 4: 1 sc in each st around. (9 sts)
Do not fasten off or stuff; press flat and sc across the top of the fin, through both sides, to close. Fasten off, leaving a tail for sewing.

FINISHING

DORSAL FIN

With the top fin pressed flat, place and pin it to the body with your yarn tail facing the front of the body. This ensures that the increases you made in Rnds 2 and 4 of the top fin are facing the back of the dolphin, giving the fin its curved appearance.

SIDE FINS

The side fins are sewn into the round directly above where the body changes from col 1 to col 2.

TAIL

Pin and sew the tail to the body using the image on the right as a guide.

Top tip

Make a pod of dolphins in shades of blue, green, and purple, and hang them from a frame to create a super cute baby mobile.

Snail, frog & log

These baby frogs and snails are quick and easy to crochet,
as is the hollow log for them to play in.

NAME: **LUCY COLLIN**

BIO: Lucy has been designing amigurumi for seven years. Her children encouraged her to use her crochet skills to make them cute toys, and she then started to sell the patterns online. She has had two books published, including *Star Wars Crochet*, and has had several patterns included in various magazines. lucyravenscar.blogspot.com/

DIFFICULTY:
★ ★ ☆ ☆ ☆

HOOK
E/4 (3.5mm) for snail and frog
G/6 (4mm) for log

YARN
For this project, we have used Stylecraft Batik. You will need DK weight yarn in your choice of colors.

Snail:
Color 1: Shell (scrap yarn)
Color 2: Body (scrap yarn)

Frog:
Color 1: Underbelly (scrap yarn)
Color 2: Body (scrap yarn)
Color 3: Eyes (scrap yarn)

Log:
Color 1: Dark wood (1 ball)
Color 2: Light wood (1 ball)

NOTIONS
Fiberfill
Black thread

MEASUREMENTS
Snail: 2¼" (5.7cm) long
Frog: 1¼" (3.2cm) long
Log: 4½" (11.4cm) long

APPROX TIME TAKEN
Less than an hour each

SPECIAL STITCH
3sc bobble stitch (3sc-bob) (see page 159)

SNAIL

SHELL
Using the hook and col 1, ch 2.
Rnd 1: 4 sc in 2nd ch from hook. (4 sts)
Rnd 2: 2 sc in each st. (8 sts)
Rnd 3 (flo): 2 sc in each st. (16 sts)
Rnd 4: (sc2tog, 1 sc in next 2 sts 4 times. (12 sts)
Rnd 5 (flo): 2 sc in each st. (24 sts)
Rnds 6–9: 1 sc in each st. (4 Rnds of 24 sts)
Rnd 10: (sc2tog, 1 sc in next 2 sts) 6 times. (18 sts)
Rnd 11: (sc2tog, 1 sc in next st) 6 times. (12 sts)
ss in next st then fasten off, leaving a long length of yarn.

BODY
Using the hook and col 2, ch 2.
Rnd 1: 6 sc in 2nd ch from hook. (6 sts)
Rnd 2: 2 sc in each st. (12 sts)
Rnd 3: 1 sc in next st, *ss in next st, ch 5, ss in second ch from hook and in next ch 3, ss back into original st at base of 5 ch (antenna made)**, 1 sc in next st, rep from * to ** to make next antenna, 1 sc in next 8 sts. (12 sts)
Rnds 4–10: 1 sc in each st. (7 Rnds of 12 sts)
ss in next st, then fasten off.

FINISHING

Stuff the shell firmly and the body lightly. Use col 3 to embroider the eyes and mouth and white yarn for highlights on the eyes. Use the yarn from the shell to sew the shell and body together. Sew a couple of stitches between the side of the shell and the body, and tighten to make the body sit more closely to the shell.

FROG

Using the hook and col 1, ch 2.
Rnd 1: 6 sc in 2nd ch from hook. (6 sts)
Rnd 2: 2 sc in each st. (12 sts)
Rnd 3: (2 sc in next st, 1 sc in next st) 6 times. (18 sts)
Rnd 4: 1 sc in next 2 sts, *ss in next st, ch 5, 1 sc in 2nd ch from hook, ss in next 3 ch, ss in original st at base of 5 ch (back leg made)*, 1 sc in next 3 sts, **ss in next st, ch 4, ss in 2nd ch from hook, ss in next 2 ch, ss

in original st at base of ch 4 (front leg made)**, 1 sc in next st, 3sc-bob in next 3 sts, 1 sc in next st, rep from ** to ** for next front leg, 1 sc in next 3 sts, rep from * to * for next back leg, 1 sc in next 2 sts. (18 sts)
Push the bobbles from the inside so they stick outward.
Rnd 5: 1 sc in each st. (18 sts)
Change to col 2.
Rnd 6: (sc2tog, 1 sc in next st) 6 times. (12 sts)
Rnd 7: (sc2tog) 6 times. (6 sts).
ss in next st and fasten off, leaving a length of yarn.

FINISHING

Embroider the eyes using col 3 by sewing three or four short horizontal lines on each side of the head, then use col 4 to sew one line across the middle. Stuff and sew up the hole at the bottom.

LOG

Using the hook and col 1 and col 2 held together, ch 21.
Row 1: 1 sc in 2nd ch from hook, 1 sc in each ch to end, turn. (20 sts)
Rows 2–13 (blo): 1 ch (not counted as a st), 1 sc in each st to end, turn. (20 sts)
Row 14 (blo): 1 sc in next 4 sts, ch 6, miss next 6 sts, 1 sc in next 10 sts, turn. (20 sts)
Row 15 (blo): 1 sc in next 10 sts, 6 sc in ch 6 space, 1 sc in next 4 sts, ch 1, turn. (20 sts)
Rows 16–26 (blo): 1 sc in each st to end, turn. (11 rows of 20 sts)
Fasten off, leaving long lengths of yarn. Sew the edges together to create a tube.

Join in both strands of yarn to the first sc of the hole on the side, and start working in the same st.
Rnd 1: (2 sc in next st, 1 sc in next st) 3 times, now work into ch on opposite side of hole (2 sc in next st, 1 sc in next st) 3 times. (18 sts)
Rnd 2: 1 sc in each st. (18 sts)
ss in next st and fasten off.
Darn in the ends.

Jumbo doll

Tie ribbons in the jumbo doll's curls to embellish this classic toy!

NAME: **AMY KEMBER**
BIO: Amy is a technical writer living in Ottawa, Canada. Her interest in crochet began when she discovered an amigurumi book in a used bookstore. After making a pig, she was instantly hooked. Since 2010, Amy has been designing and selling her own amigurumi patterns on Etsy.
www.etsy.com/shop/AmysGurumis/

DIFFICULTY:
★ ★ ★ ★ ☆

HOOK
F/5 (3.75mm)

YARN
In this project, we have used Bernat Handicrafter Cotton. You will need to use DK weight yarn in your chosen colors.
Color 1: Skin (3 balls)
Color 2: Hair (1 ball)
Color 3: Dress (2 balls)
Color 4: Shoes (1 ball)

NOTIONS
1 pair 10mm oval safety eyes
Yarn needle
Fiberfill
Black yarn

MEASUREMENTS
14¼" (36.2cm) tall

APPROX TIME TAKEN
15 hours

JUMBO DOLL

HEAD
Using the hook and col 1, make a magic ring.
Rnd 1: 6 sc into ring and pull it closed. (6 sts)
Rnd 2: 2 sc in each sc. (12 sts)
Rnd 3: (1 sc in next sc, 2 sc in next sc) times. (18 sts)
Rnd 4: (1 sc in each of next 2 sc, 2 sc in next sc) 6 times. (24 sts)
Rnd 5: (1 sc in each of next 3 sc, 2 sc in next sc) 6 times. (30 sts)
Rnd 6: (1 sc in each of next 4 sc, 2 sc in next sc) 6 times. (36 sts)
Rnd 7: (1 sc in each of next 5 sc, 2 sc in next sc) 6 times. (42 sts)
Rnd 8: (1 sc in each of next 6 sc, 2 sc in next sc) 6 times. (48 sts)
Rnds 9–20: 1 sc in each sc. (12 Rnds of 48 sts)
Rnd 21: (1 sc in each of next 6 sc, sc2tog in next 2 sc) 6 times. (42 sts)
Rnd 22: (1 sc in each of next 5 sc, sc2tog in next 2 sc) 6 times. (36 sts)
Rnd 23: (1 sc in each of next 4 sc, sc2tog in next 2 sc) 6 times. (30 sts)
Rnd 24: (1 sc in each of next 3 sc, sc2tog in next 2 sc) 6 times. (24 sts)
Rnd 25: (1 sc in each of next 2 sc, sc2tog in next 2 sc) 6 times. (18 sts)
Fasten off.

BODY
Using col 1, make a magic ring.
Rnd 1: 6 sc into ring and pull it closed. (6 sts)
Rnd 2: 2 sc in each sc. (12 sts)
Rnd 3: (1 sc in next sc, 2 sc in next sc) 6 times. (18 sts)
Rnd 4: (1 sc in each of next 2 sc, 2 sc in next sc) 6 times. (24 sts)
Rnd 5: (1 sc in each of next 3 sc, 2 sc in next sc) 6 times. (30 sts)
Rnd 6: (1 sc in each of next 4 sc, 2 sc in next sc) 6 times. (36 sts)
Rnd 7: (1 sc in each of next 5 sc, 2 sc in next sc) 6 times. (42 sts)
Rnds 8–19: 1 sc in each sc. (12 Rnds of 42 sts)
Rnd 20: (1 sc in each of next 5 sc, sc2tog in next 2 sc) 6 times. (36 sts)
Rnds 21–23: 1 sc in each sc. (3 Rnds of 36 sts)

Rnd 24: (1 sc in each of next 4 sc, sc2tog in next 2 sc) 6 times. (30 sts)
Rnds 25–26: 1 sc in each sc. (2 Rnds of 30 sts)
Rnd 27: (1 sc in each of next 3 sc, sc2tog in next 2 sc) 6 times. (24 sts)
Fasten off.

ARMS (MAKE 2)
Using col 1, make a magic ring.
Rnd 1: 5 sc into ring and pull it closed. (5 sts)
Rnd 2: 2 sc in each sc. (10 sts)
Rnd 3–6: 1 sc in each sc. (4 Rnds of 10 sts)
Rnd 7: (sc2tog in next 2 sc) 5 times. (5 sts)
Rnd 8: 2 sc in each sc. (10 sts)
Rnds 9–23: 1 sc in each sc. (16 Rnds of 10 sts)
Fasten off.

LEGS (MAKE 2)
Using col 1, make a magic ring.
Rnd 1: 6 sc into ring and pull it closed. (6 sts)
Rnd 2: 2 sc in each sc. (12 sts)
Rnd 3: (2 sc in each of next 3 sc, 1 sc in each of next 3 sc) twice. (18 sts)
Rnd 4: (1 sc in next sc, 2 sc in next sc) 3 times, 1 sc in each of next 3 sc, (1 sc in next sc, 2 sc in next sc) 3 times, 1 sc in each of next 3 sc. (24 sts)
Rnd 5–6: 1 sc in each sc. (2 Rnds of 24 sts)
Rnd 7: 1 dc in each of next 12 sc, 1 sc in each of next 12 sc. (24 sts)
Rnd 8: (sc2tog in next 2 dc) 6 times, 1 sc in each of next 12 sc. (18 sts)
Rnds 9–28: 1 sc in each sc. (20 Rnds of 18 sts)
Fasten off.

HAIR
Using col 2, make a magic ring.
Rnd 1: 6 sc into ring and pull it closed. (6 sts)
Rnd 2: 2 sc in each sc. (12 sts)
Rnd 3: (1 sc in next sc, 2 sc in next sc) 6 times. (18 sts)
Rnd 4: (1 sc in each of next 2 sc, 2 sc in next sc) 6 times. (24 sts)
Rnd 5: (1 sc in each of next 3 sc, 2 sc in next sc) 6 times. (30 sts)
Rnd 6: (1 sc in each of next 4 sc, 2 sc in next sc) 6 times. (36 sts)
Rnd 7: (1 sc in each of next 5 sc, 2 sc in next sc) 6 times. (42 sts)

Rnd 8: (1 sc in each of next 6 sc, 2 sc in next sc) 6 times. (48 sts)

Rnd 9 (transition from rnds to rows): (5 dc in next sc, skip next sc, 1 ss in next sc, skip next sc) 4 times, 1 dc in each of next 32 sc, turn. (4 scallops and 32 sts)

Rows 10–12: ch 1, 1 sc in each sc, turn. (leaving bangs unworked) (3 rows of 32 sts)

FORM CURLS

Row 13: *ch 16, beg with 2nd ch from hook, 1 ss in each of next ch 15, skip 1 sc, ss in next *Fix odd line break last st, ch 16, beg with 2nd ch from hook, 1 ss in each of next 15 ch, ss in last sc. (16 curls made)
Fasten off, leaving a long tail.

DRESS

Using col 3, ch 36.
Row 1: 1 sc into 2nd ch from hook, 1 sc in each ch, turn. (35 sts)
Row 2: ch 1, (1 sc in each of next 4 sc, 2 sc in next sc) 6 times, 1 sc in each of next 5 sc, turn. (41 sts)
Row 3: ch 1, (1 sc in each of next 5 sc, 2 sc in next sc) 6 times, 1 sc in each of next 5 sc, turn. (47 sts)
Row 4: ch 1, 1 sc in each sc, turn. (47 sts)

Row 5 (Make sleeves): ch 1, 1 sc in each of next 8 sc, ch 3 and skip 7 sc, join in 16th sc with ss, 1 sc in each of next 15 sc, ch 3 and skip 7 sc, join in 38th sc with ss, 1 sc in each of next 8 sc, turn. (37 sts)

NOTE: Do not count the ss from this Rnd as sts in the following Rnd.

Row 6: ch 1, 1 sc in each sc, turn. (37 sts)
Row 7: ch 1, 1 sc in each of next 6 sc, 2 sc in next sc, (1 sc in each of next 5 sc, 2 sc in next sc) 4 times, 1 sc in each of next 6 sc, do not turn. (42 sts)
Join with ss and begin working in rnds.
Rnds 8–13: 1 sc in each sc. (6 Rnds of 42 sts)
Rnd 14: (1 dc in next sc, 2 dc in next sc) 21 times. (63 sts)
Rnds 15–21: 1 dc in each dc. (7 Rnds of 63 sts)
Rnd 22: 1 dc in each dc to last 5 sts, 1 hdc in each of next 2 dc, 1 sc in each of next 2 dc, ss into last dc. (Avoids jog at join)

ASSEMBLE THE DRESS

Cut a strand of yarn that is several feet long, and secure it to the top right of the opening at the back of the dress.

Using that strand, ch 3 and ss into the 1st st at the top of the dress (to form the buttonhole), then continue to ss along the opening of the dress until you reach the opposite side of the opening and fasten off.

Using the other yarn end on the left side of the dress opening, fasten a white button to the dress and weave in the ends.

SHOES (MAKE 2)

Using col 4, make a magic ring.

Rnd 1: 6 sc into ring and pull it closed. (6 sts)

Rnd 2: 2 sc in each sc. (12 sts)

Rnd 3: (2 sc in each of next 3 sc, 1 sc in each of next 3 sc) twice. (18 sts)

Rnd 4: (1 sc in next sc, 2 sc in next sc) 3 times, 1 sc in each of next 3 sc, (1 sc in next sc, 2 sc in next sc) 3 times, 1 sc in each of next 3 sc. (24 sts)

Rnds 5–7: 1 sc in each sc. (3 Rnds of 24 sts)

Rnd 8: 1 dc in each of next 12 sc, 1 sc in each of next 12 sc. (24 sts)

Rnd 9: (sc2tog in the next 2 dc) 6 times, 1 sc in each of next 12 sc. (18 sts)

MAKE SHOE STRAP:

Ch 7, skip 5 sc, join in 7th sc with ss.
Fasten off.

ASSEMBLE THE FACE

Insert the oval safety eyes between Rnd 15 and Rnd 16 of the head, and position them six stitches apart.

Embroider a V-shaped mouth on Rnd 18 using a yarn needle and black yarn.
Stuff the head firmly.

FINISHING

Stuff the body, arms, and legs.
Sew the body to the head—there is one extra decrease Rnd on the head than on the body so the last Rnd of the body (Rnd 26) should be sewn around the second to last Rnd on the head (Rnd 23).

Sew the hair to the head (stitch up the side of the head, above the bangs, down the other side of the head, and then in between the hair piece and the curls along the back).
Sew the arms to the body between Rnd 26 and Rnd 27, and position them nine stitches apart in the front.

Sew the legs to the body between Rnd 4 and Rnd 5, and position them right next to each other in the front (with no stitches in between).

Baby guinea pigs

Quick to make and using minimal amounts of yarn, these little cuties would be perfect for last-minute gifts, stocking fillers, or party favors.

NAME: **KATI GÁLUSZ**

BIO: Kati is an amigurumi designer from Hungary. She loves to create patterns for realistic animals, and for her favorite movie and TV characters. www.ravelry.com/designers/kati-galusz

DIFFICULTY:
★ ★ ★ ☆ ☆

HOOK
C/2 or D/3 (3mm)

YARN
In this project, we have used Red Heart yarn. You will need a DK weight yarn in your chosen colors. See the individual designs on the following pages to determine how many colors you need for each and where those colors will be used.

NOTIONS
Stitch marker
1 pair 7.5mm safety eyes
Fiberfill
Yarn needle
Wire cutter (optional)

MEASUREMENTS
2"–2¼" (5.1–5.7cm) long,
1¼"–1½" (3.2–3.8cm) tall

APPROX TIME TAKEN
1 hour per guinea pig

SPECIAL STITCH
4dc-bobble stitch (4dc-bob) (see page 159)

TAN GUINEA PIG

HEAD AND BODY
Using the hook and col 1, make a magic ring.
Rnd 1: 6 sc in magic ring, pull ring tight to close. (6 sts)
Rnd 2: (2 sc in next st, 1 sc in next st) 3 times. (9 sts)
Rnd 3: (2 sc in next st, 1 sc in next st) 3 times, 1 sc in next 3 sts. (12 sts)
Rnd 4: (2 sc in next st, 1 sc in next 2 sts) 3 times, 1 sc in next 3 sts. (15 sts)
Rnd 5: 1 sc in each st around. (15 sts)
Rnd 6: 1 sc in next 5 sts, 2 sc in next st, 1 sc in next 5 sts, 2 sc in next st, 1 sc in next 2 sts, 2 sc in next st. (18 sts)
Rnd 7: 1 sc in next 13 sts, 2 sc in next st, 1 sc in next 2 sts, 2 sc in next st, 1 sc in next st. (20 sts)
Rnd 8: 1 sc in next 14 sts, 4dc-bob in next st, 1 sc in next 2 sts, 4dc-bob in next st, 1 sc in next 2 sts. (20 sts)
Rnd 9: 1 sc in next 5 sts, sc2tog, 1 sc in next 13 sts. (19 sts)
Rnd 10: 1 sc in each st around. (19 sts)

Next, insert the safety eyes between Rnds 4 and 5 on either side of the head, six to seven stitches apart. If the eye stems are too long for the tiny head, use a wire cutter to chop off a bit of the length so they fit in comfortably. Stuff the head, making sure that the stuffing gets all the way to the nose, beyond the eye stems.

Rnd 11: 1 sc in next 6 sts, 2 sc in next st, 1 sc in next 12 sts. (20 sts)
Rnd 12: 1 sc in each st around. (20 sts)
Rnd 13: 1 sc in next 4 sts, sc2tog, 1 sc in next 2 sts, sc2tog, 1 sc in next 10 sts. (18 sts)
Rnd 14: 1 sc in next 3 sts, sc2tog, 1 sc in next 2 sts, sc2tog, 1 sc in next 9 sts. (16 sts)
Rnd 15: (Invdec, 1 sc in next 2 sts) 4 times. (12 sts)
Stuff body firmly.
Rnd 16: (Invdec) 6 times. (6 sts)

Before fastening off, check that your guinea pig can sit. If it falls on its nose, try pushing a little more stuffing into the bottom, and pull the bobble stitches outward so the front legs stick out more.
Once you are happy with your guinea pig, fasten off and use the yarn end to close the remaining hole.

EARS (MAKE 2)
Using col 2, make a magic ring.
Rnd 1: ch 2, (1 hdc, 2 sc, 1 hdc) into the ring, ch 2, ss into the ring. Cut the yarn leaving a long end, and fasten off. Tighten the ring.
Sew the ears to the head: they should lay flat on the head and nearly touch the eyes.

REAR FEET (MAKE 2)
Using col 1, ch 5.
Row 1: 1 sc in second ch from hook and in the next 3 ch, turn. (4 sts)
Row 2: ch 1 (not counted as a st), 1 sc in each st to end, turn. (4 sts)
Row 3: ch 1, fold the piece in half lengthwise and line up the free edge of the beginning chain with the stitches of Row 2. Working through both layers, ss in next 4 sts. Fasten off, leaving a long yarn end.

FINISHING

Place the legs beside the body—the tips should be 1–2 Rnds behind the front legs, with yarn tails near the bottom. Sew this end to the guinea pig, then make a few stitches at the middle of the leg to anchor it safely to the body.

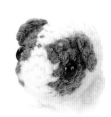

BROWN AND TAN GUINEA PIG

HEAD AND BODY
Follow the instructions as for the tan guinea pig for Rnds 1–7.
Rnd 8: 1 sc in next 14 sts, 4dc-bob, 1 sc in next st, change to col 2, 1 sc in next st, 4dc-bob in next st, 1 sc in next 2 sts.
Rnd 9: 1 sc in next 4 sts, change to col 1, 1 sc in next st, sc2tog, 1 sc in next 7 sts, change to col 2, 1 sc in next 6 sts. (19 sts)
Rnd 10: 1 sc in next 7 sts, change to col 1, 1 sc in next 5 sts, change to col 2, 1 sc in next (7 sts)

Insert the safety eyes between Rnds 4 and 5 on either side of the head, six to seven stitches apart. If the eye stems are too long for the tiny head, use a wire cutter to chop off a bit of the length so they fit in comfortably. Stuff the head, making sure that the stuffing gets all the way to the nose, beyond the eye stems.

Rnd 11: 1 sc in next 6 sts, 2 sc in next st, 1 sc in next st, change to col 1, 1 sc in next 3 sts, change to col 2, 1 sc in next 8 sts. (20 sts)
Rnd 12: 1 sc in next 9 sts, change to col 1, 1 sc in next 2 sts, change to col 2, 1 sc in next 9 sts.
Rnd 13: 1 sc in next 4 sts, sc2tog, 1 sc in next 2 sts, sc2tog, 1 sc in next 10 sts. (18 sts)
Rnd 14: 1 sc in next 3 sts, sc2tog, 1 sc in next 2 sts, sc2tog, 1 sc in next 2 sts, change to col 1, 1 sc in next 7 sts. (16 sts)
Rnds 15–16: Follow the instructions given for the tan guinea pig.

EARS AND REAR FEET
Follow the the instructions given for the tan guinea pig using col 1 for each piece.

GRAY AND WHITE GUINEA PIG

HEAD AND BODY
Using the hook and col 2, make a magic ring.
Rnd 1 (RS): 6 sc in magic ring, pull ring tight to close. (6 sts)
Rnd 2: 2 sc in next st, 1 sc in next st, change to col 1, (2 sc in next st, 1 sc in next st) twice. (9 sts)
Rnd 3: 2 sc in next st, change to col 2, 1 sc in next st, 2 sc in next st, change to col 1, 1 sc in next st, 2 sc in next st, 1 sc in next 4 sts. (12 sts)
Rnd 4: 2 sc in next st, 1 sc in next st, change to col 2, 1 sc in next st, 2 sc in next st, 1 sc in next st, change to col 1, 1 sc in next st, 2 sc in next st, 1 sc in next 5 sts. (15 sts)
Rnd 5: 1 sc in next 3 sts, change to col 2, 1 sc in next 4 sts, change to col 1, 1 sc in next 8 sts. (15 sts)
Rnd 6: 1 sc in next 4 sts, change to col 2, 1 sc in next st, 2 sc in next st, change to col 1, 1 sc in next 5 sts, 2 sc in next st, 1 sc in next 2 sts, 2 sc in next st. (18 sts)
Rnds 7–16: Follow the instructions given for the tan guinea pig.

EARS AND REAR FEET
Follow the instructions given for the tan guinea pig using col 1 for each piece.

TRICOLOR GUINEA PIG

HEAD AND BODY

Rnds 1–7: Follow the instructions given for the tan guinea pig. (20 sts)

Rnd 8: 1 sc in next 6 sts, change to col 2, 1 sc in next 8 sts, 4dc-bob in next st, 1 sc in next 2 sts, 4dc-bob in next st, 1 sc in next 2 sts.

Rnd 9: 1 sc in next 5 sts, sc2tog, 1 sc in next 13 sts. (19 sts)

Rnd 10: 1 sc in each st around. (19 sts)

Insert the safety eyes between Rnds 4 and 5 on either side of the head, six to seven stitches apart. If the eye stems are too long for the tiny head, use a wire cutter to chop off a bit of the length so they fit in comfortably. Stuff the head, making sure that the stuffing gets all the way to the nose, beyond the eye stems.

Rnd 11: 1 sc in next 4 sts, change to col 3, 1 sc in next 2 sts, 2 sc in next st, 1 sc in next 5 sts, change to col 2, 1 sc in next 7 sts. (20 sts)

Rnd 12: 1 sc in next 2 sts, change to col 3, 1 sc in next 18 sts. (20 sts)

Rnd 13: 1 sc in next 4 sts, sc2tog, 1 sc in next 2 sts, sc2tog, 1 sc in next 10 sts. (18 sts)

Rnd 14: Change to col 1, 1 sc in next 3 sts, sc2tog, 1 sc in next st, change to col 3, 1 sc in next st, sc2tog, 1 sc in next 5 sts, change to col 1, 1 sc in next 4 sts. (16 sts)

Rnds 15–16: Follow instructions given for the tan guinea pig.

EARS

Follow the instructions given for the tan guinea pig using col 1.

REAR FEET

Follow the instructions given for the tan guinea pig using col 1 for one foot and col 2 for the other. Attach each foot to the side where its col is the more dominant.

WHITE AND BROWN GUINEA PIG

HEAD AND BODY

Using the hook and col 1, make a magic ring.

Rnd 1 (RS): 6 sc in magic ring, pull ring tight to close. (6 sts)

Rnd 2: (2 sc in next st, 1 sc in next st) twice, 2 sc in next st, change to col 2, 1 sc in next st. (9 sts)

Rnd 3: 1 sc in next st, 2 sc in next st, change to col 1, 1 sc in next st, change to col 2, 2 sc in next st, 1 sc in next 2 sts, change to col 1, 2 sc in next st, 1 sc in next st, change to col 2, 1 sc in next st. (12 sts)

Rnd 4: 2 sc in next st, 1 sc in next 2 sts, change to col 1, 2 sc in next st, change to col 2, 1 sc in next 2 sts, 2 sc in next st, 1 sc in next st, change to col 1, 1 sc in next 3 sts, change to col 2, 1 sc in next st. (15 sts)

Rnd 5: 1 sc in next 4 sts, change to col 1, 1 sc in next 2 sts, change to col 2, 1 sc in next 5 sts, change to col 1, 1 sc in next 3 sts, change to col 2, 1 sc in next st. (15 sts)

Rnd 6: 1 sc in next 4 sts, change to col 1, 1 sc in next st, 2 sc in next st, change to col 2, 1 sc in next 5 sts, change to col 1, 2 sc in next st, 1 sc in next 3 sts, change to col 2, 1 sc in the same st as previous sc. (18 sts)

Rnd 7: 1 sc in next 3 sts, change to col 1, 1 sc in next 5 sts, change to col 2, 1 sc in next 4 sts, change to col 1, (1 sc in next st, 2 sc in next st, 1 sc in next st) twice. (20 sts)

Rnds 8–16: Follow the instructions given for the tan guinea pig.

EARS AND REAR FEET

Follow the instructions given for the tan guinea pig.

Flemish giant rabbit

Bring favorite characters or childhood pets to life
by learning how to create a realistic rabbit.

NAME: **KATI GÁLUSZ**

BIO: Kati is an amigurumi designer from Hungary. She loves to create patterns for realistic animals, and for her favorite movie and television characters.
www.ravelry.com/designers/kati-galusz

DIFFICULTY:
★ ★ ★ ☆ ☆

HOOK
C/2 or D/3 (3mm)

YARN
In this project, we have used Schachenmayr Bravo. You will need a DK weight yarn in your chosen colors.
Color 1: Body (1 ball)
Color 2: Tail (1 ball)

NOTIONS
Stitch marker
1 pair 12mm safety eyes
Fiberfill
Yarn needle
Wire brush (optional)
Embroidery floss and needle

MEASUREMENTS
8 ¾" (22.2cm) long, 4" (10.2cm) tall without ears

APPROX TIME TAKEN
5 hours

FLEMISH GIANT RABBIT

FRONT LEGS (MAKE 2)
Using the hook and col 1, make a magic ring.
Rnd 1: 6 sc into magic ring, pull ring tight to close. (6 sts)
Rnd 2: 2 sc in each st. (12 sts)
Rnds 3–7: 1 sc in each st. ss into next st and fasten off. (4 Rnds of 12 sts)

HEAD AND BODY
Using col 1, make a magic ring.
Rnd 1: 6 sc into magic ring, pull ring tight to close. (6 sts)
Rnd 2: 2 sc in each st. (12 sts)
Rnd 3: (2 sc in next st, 1 sc in next st) 6 times. (18 sts)
Rnd 4: 1 sc in each st. (18 sts)
Rnd 5: (2 sc in next st, 1 sc in next 2 sts) 6 times. (24 sts)
Rnd 6: 1 sc in each st. (24 st)
Rnd 7: (2 sc in next st, 1 sc in next 3 sts) 6 times. (30 sts)
Rnds 8–9: 1 sc in each st. (2 Rnds of 30 sts)
Rnd 10: (2 sc in next st, 1 sc in next 4 sts) 6 times. (36 sts)
Rnds 11–13: 1 sc in each st. (3 Rnds of 36 sts)
Rnd 14: (1 sc in next st, 2 sc in next st) 3 times, 1 sc in next 7 sts, (2 sc in next st, sc in next 6 sts) 3 times, 1 sc in next 2 sts. (42 sts)
Rnd 15: (2 sc in next st, 1 sc in next 2 sts) 3 times, sc in next 33 sts. (45 sts)

Join the front legs to the body in the next rnd.

Rnd 16: 1 sc in next st, then join as follows: hold a leg in front of the body and crochet through both layers, 1 sc in next 4 sts, continue working on the body only, 1 sc in next 3 sts, hold the second leg in front of the body and working through both layers, 1 sc in next 4 sts, continue on body only, 1 sc in next 33 sts. (45 sts)
Rnd 17: 1 sc in next st, then work as follows:

Skip the 4 joining sc and instead work 1 sc in each of the 8 unworked leg sts from the last rnd, 1 sc in next 3 sts between the legs, skip the next 4 joining sts and work 1 sc in next 8 unworked sts of second leg, continuing on the body, 1 sc in next 13 sts, sc2tog, 1 sc in next 3 sts, sc2tog, 1 sc in next 13 sts. (51 sts)

Rnd 18: 2 sc in next st, 1 sc in next 7 sts, sc2tog, 1 sc in next st, sc2tog, 1 sc in next 7 sts, 2 sc in next st, 1 sc in next 14 sts, sc2tog, 1 sc in next 14 sts. (50 sts)
Rnd 19: 1 sc in next 32 sts, sc2tog, 1 sc in next 3 sts, sc2tog, 1 sc in next 11 sts. (48 sts)

Rnd 20: 1 sc in next 31 sts, sc2tog, 1 sc in next 3 sts, sc2tog, 1 sc in next 10 sts. (46 sts)
Rnd 21: 1 sc in next 33 sts, sc2tog, 1 sc in next 11 sts. (45 sts)

Stuff the head and front legs and place (do not fix) the safety eyes between Rnds 9 and 10, approximately 12 sts apart. Remove the stuffing, then fix the eyes in place following the manufacturer's instructions.
Rnds 22–28: 1 sc in each st. (7 Rnds of 45 sts)
Rnd 29: 1 sc in next 32 sts, (2 sc in next st, 1 sc in next 2 sts) 3 times, sc in next 4 sts. (48 sts)
Rnd 30: 1 sc in next 34 sts, 2 sc in next st, 1 sc in next 4 sts, 2 sc in next st, 1 sc in each of next 8 sts. (50 sts)
Rnds 31–32: 1 sc in each st.
Rnd 33: 1 sc in next 35 sts, 2 sc in next st, 1 sc in next 5 sts, 2 sc in next st, 1 sc in next 8 sts. (52 sts)
Rnds 34–35: 1 sc in each st.

Note: You need to start Rnd 36 at the middle of the belly, so before continuing with Rnd 36, make sure you work 1 sc in as many sts as necessary to be in the correct position (this will help to make the haunches symmetrical).

Rnd 36: 1 sc in next 6 sts, 2 scflo in next 8 sts, 1 sc in next 24 sts, 2 scflo in next 8 sts, 1 sc in next 6 sts. (68 sts)
Rnd 37: 1 sc in next 31 sts, 2 sc in next st, 1 sc in next 4 sts, 2 sc in next st, 1 sc in next 31 sts. (70 sts)
Rnd 38: 1 sc in next 7 sts, (sc2tog, 1 sc in next st) 5 times, 1 sc in next 26 sts, (1 sc in next st, sc2tog) 5 times, 1 sc in next 7 sts. (60 sts)
Rnds 39–43: 1 sc in each st. (5 Rnds of 60 sts)
Stuff the head, front legs, and shoulders.
Rnd 44: 1 sc in next 24 sts, (sc2tog, 1 sc in next 4 sts) 3 times, 1 sc in next 18 sts. (57 sts)
Rnds 45–46: 1 sc in each st. (2 Rnds of 57 sts)
Rnd 47: 1 sc in next 24 sts, (sc2tog, 1 sc in next 3 sts) 3 times, 1 sc in next 18 sts. (54 sts)
Rnds 48–49: 1 sc in each st. (2 Rnds of 54 sts)
Rnd 50: (1 sc in next 8 sts, sc2tog, 1 sc in next 8 sts) 3 times. (51 sts)
Rnd 51: (sc2tog, 1 sc in next 15 sts) 3 times. (48 sts)
Rnd 52: (1 sc in next 3 sts, sc2tog, 1 sc in next 3 sts) 6 times. (42 sts)
Rnd 53: (sc2tog, 1 sc in next 5 sts) 6 times. (36 sts)
Rnd 54: (1 sc in next 2 sts, sc2tog, 1 sc in next 2 sts) 6 times. (30 sts)
Rnd 55: (sc2tog, 1 sc in next 3 sts) 6 times. (24 sts)

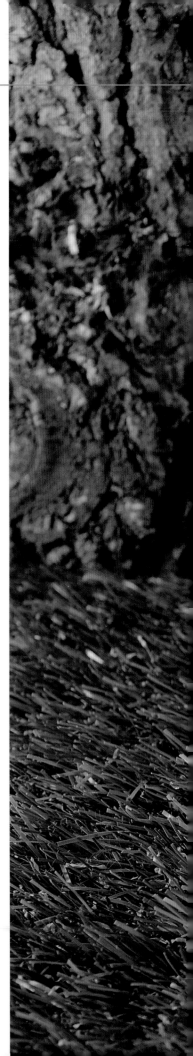

Rnd 56: (1 sc in next st, sc2tog, 1 sc in next st) 6 times. (18 sts)
Start stuffing the body, making sure the stuffing is evenly distributed and emphasizes the semi-arched backline.

Rnd 57: (sc2tog, 1 sc in next st) 6 times. (12 sts)
Add a little more fiberfill if necessary.

Rnd 58: (sc2tog) 6 times. (6 sts) ss in next st, fasten off, and use yarn end to close the remaining gap.

EARS (MAKE 2)
Using col 1, make a magic ring.
Rnd 1: 6 sc into magic ring, pull ring tight to close. (6 sts)
Rnd 2: (2 sc in next st, 1 sc in next 2 sts) twice. (8 sts)
Rnd 3: (2 sc in next st, 1 sc in next 3 sts) twice. (10 sts)
Rnd 4: (2 sc in next st, 1 sc in next 4 sts) twice. (12 sts)
Rnd 5: 1 sc in each st. (12 sts)
Rnd 6: (2 sc in next st, 1 sc in next 5 sts) twice. (14 sts)
Rnd 7: 1 sc in each st. (14 sts)
Rnd 8: (2 sc in next st, 1 sc in next 6 sts) twice. (16 sts)
Rnd 9: 1 sc in each st. (16 sts)
Rnd 10: (2 sc in next st, 1 sc in next 7 sts) twice. (18 sts)
Rnd 11: 1 sc in each st. (18 sts)
Rnd 12: (2 sc in next st, 1 sc in next 8 sts) twice. (20 sts)
Rnd 13: 1 sc in each st. (20 sts)
Rnd 14: (2 sc in next st, 1 sc in next 9 sts) twice. (22 sts)
Rnds 15–20: 1 sc in each st. (6 Rnds of 22 sts)

ss into next st and fasten off, leaving a long yarn end.

Flatten the ear, pinch together the bottom corners, then sew them together to fix the ear in this position. The ears will define your bunny's personality. Sew them to the head in that position.

REAR FEET (MAKE 2)
Using col 1, make a magic ring.
Rnd 1: 6 sc into magic ring, pull ring tight to close. (6 sts)
Rnd 2: 2 sc in each st. (12 sts)
Rnds 3–15: 1 sc in each st. (13 Rnds or 12 sts)
Rnd 16: (sc2tog) 4 times, leaving remaining 4 sts unworked. (4 sts) ss in next st and fasten off, leaving a long yarn end.

The rear feet bear no weight, so you can stuff them lightly. Pin them to the body at ground level, just forward of the "haunches." Flatten the open ends to the body and sew to the body, then make a few sts between the body and feet about halfway forward so they stay in the right place.

TAIL
Using col 2, make a magic ring.
Rnd 1: 6 sc into magic ring, pull ring tight to close. (6 sts)
Rnd 2: 2 sc in each st. (12 sts)
Rnd 3: (2 sc in next st, 1 sc in next 3 sts) 3 times. (15 sts)
Rnds 4–7: 1 sc in each st. (2 Rnds of 15 sts)
Rnd 8: (sc2tog, 1 sc in next 3 sts) 3 times. (12 sts)
Rnd 9: (sc2tog, 1 sc in next st) 4 times. (8 sts)

ss into next st and fasten off, leaving a long end.

Stuff the tail lightly so it's rounded, but still flat. The closed tip of the tail should be placed where you closed the last Rnd of the body. Flatten the bottom end of the tail, then sew it to the body, closing the gap in the process. Then make a few sts between the body and tail to anchor it in the right position.
If you want a fuzzy tail, brush the tail with a wire brush until it becomes fluffy.

FINISHING

Using six strands of floss and a pointed embroidery needle, embroider the nose and the mouth.

Top tip!
As you become more confident, try adding color changes so you can replicate your beloved pet.

Soccer captain

Create a miniature soccer player with trophy and soccer accessories.
You can even change colors to match a favorite team!

NAME: **KATRINA EVANS**
BIO: Katrina enjoys creating lifelike miniatures with character and style. She has developed a special interest in custom-made crocheted pets from photos, her greyhounds and whippets have proved especially popular and have been ordered by customers in the UK and Europe.

www.etsy.com/uk/shop/KatyJaneCreations

DIFFICULTY:
★ ★ ★ ☆ ☆

HOOK
B/1 (2mm)

YARN
In this project, we have used King Cole 4-ply Bamboo.
You will need to use super fine weight yarn in your chosen colors.
Color 1: Skin (1 ball)
Color 2: Shoe soles (scrap yarn)
Color 3: Shoes (scrap yarn)
Color 4: White (1 ball)
Color 5: Hair (scrap yarn)
Color 6: Shirt (1 ball)
Color 7: Black (scrap yarn)
Color 8: Trophy (scrap yarn)

NOTIONS
Yarn needle
Fiberfill
Black & red thread

MEASUREMENTS
7 ¾" (19.7cm) tall, depending on hook and yarn size used

APPROX TIME TAKEN
About 10 hours

SOCCER CAPTAIN

HEAD
Using the hook and col 1, make a magic ring.
Rnd 1: 6 sc into the ring and pull it closed. (6 sts)
Rnd 2: 2 sc in each sc. (12 sts)
Rnd 3: (1 sc in next sc, 2 sc in next sc) 6 times. (18 sts)
Rnd 4: (1 sc in each of next 2 sc, 2 sc in next sc) 6 times. (24 sts)
Rnd 5: (1 sc in each of next 3 sc, 2 sc in next sc) 6 times. (30 sts)
Rnds 6–13: 1 sc in each sc. (8 Rnds of 30 sts)
Rnd 14: (1 sc in each of next 3 sc, sc2tog in next 2 sc) 6 times. (24 sts)
Rnd 15: (1 sc in each of next 2 sc, sc2tog in next 2 sc) 6 times. (18 sts)
Lightly stuff.
Rnd 16: (1 sc in next sc, sc2tog in next 2 sc) 6 times. (12 sts)
Rnd 17: (1 sc in next 2 sc, sc2tog in next 2 sc) 3 times. (9 sts)
Rnd 18: 1 sc in each sc. (9 sts)
Fasten off.

SHOES, SOCKS, AND LEGS
FIRST LEG
Using col 2, ch 5.
Rnd 1: 2 sc into 2nd ch from hook, 1 sc in each of next ch 2, 4 sc in next ch, rotate work to cont along bottom of ch, 1 sc in each of next ch 2, 4 sc in next ch. (14 sts)
Rnd 2: 2 sc in next sc, 1 sc in each of next 3 sc, 2 hdc in each of next 4 sc, 1 sc in each of next 3 sc, 2 sc in each of next 3 sc. (22 sts)

Note: You should now be at the heel of the foot.

Change to col 3.
Rnd 3 (flo): 1 sc in each st. (22 sts)
Rnd 4: 1 sc in each of next 9 sc, (sc2tog in next 2 sc) twice, 1 sc in each of next 9 sc. (20 sts)
Rnd 5: 1 sc in each of next 6 sc, 1 hdc in each of next 8 hdc, 1 sc in each of next 6 sc. (20 sts)
Rnd 6: 1 sc in each of next 6 sc, (sc2tog in next 2 hdc) 4 times, 1 sc in each of next 6 sc. (16 sts)
Change to col 4.
Rnd 7 (flo): 1 sc in each of next 5 sc, (sc2tog in next 2 sc) 3 times, 1 sc in each of next 5 sc. (13 sts)
Rnd 8: 1 sc in each of next 4 sc, (sc2tog in next 2 sc) twice, 1 sc in each of next 5 sc. (11 sts)
Stuff the foot, and continue to leg.
Rnd 9: 1 sc in each of next 4 sc, sc2tog in next 2 sc, 1 sc in each of next 5 sc. (10 sts)
Rnd 10: 1 sc in each of next 3 sc, (sc2tog in next 2 sc) twice, 1 sc in each of next 3 sc. (8 sts)
Rnd 11–14 (flo): 1 sc in each sc. (4 Rnds of 8 sts)
Rnd 15 (flo): 2 sc in next sc, 1 sc in each of next 6 sc, 2 sc in next sc. (10 sts)
Rnds 16–18 (flo): 1 sc in each sc. (3 Rnds of 10 sts)
Change to col 1.
Rnd 19 (flo): sc2tog in next 2 sc, 1 sc in each of next 3 sc, 2 sc in each of next 2 sc, 1 sc in each of next 3 sc. (11 sts)

Rnd 20: 1 sc in each of next 5 sc, 1 hdc in next 4 sc, 1 sc in each of next 2 sc. (11 sts)
Stuff lower leg.
Rnd 21: 1 sc in each st. (11 sts)
Rnd 22: 1 sc in each of next 5 sc, 2 sc in each of next sc, 1 sc in each of next 5 sc. (12 sts)
Rnd 23: (2 sc in next sc, 1 sc in each of next 5 sc) twice. (14 sts)
Rnds 24–33: 1 sc in each sc. (10 Rnds of 14 sts)
Fasten off, adding more stuffing, if needed, twist leg a little until foot and knee are facing in same direction.

SECOND LEG
Work Rnds 1–33 as for first leg but do not fasten off.
Stuff both legs, then hold the first leg next to the second one in position, making sure the knees are facing the same way, with the feet toward you. Make sure the yarn is on the far right side of the doll by your right hand, still on the second leg.

JOIN LEGS
With the legs held side-by-side and squeezed flat along the tops, ch 1, 1 sc in each sc straight across the first leg through two thicknesses, then continue across the other leg to join them as one piece, turn. (14st—7 sc for each leg)
Rnd 34: ch 1, 1 sc in each of next 14 sc along the back loops, then turn and continue working 1 sc in each of next 14 sc in front loops. (28 sts)
Rnd 35: 1 sc in each sc. (28 sts)
Rnd 36: 1 sc in each of next 2 sc, 2 sc in next sc, (1 sc in next sc, 2 sc in next sc) 3 times, 1 sc in each of next 19 sc. (32 sts)

Rnd 37: (sc2tog in next 2 sc, 1 sc in each of next 2 sc) 3 times, sc2tog in next 2 sc, 1 dec in each of next 18 sc. (28 sts)
Rnd 38: (sc2tog in next 2 sc, 1 sc in each of next 5 sc) 3 times, sc2tog in next 2 sc, 1 sc in each of next 5 sc. (24 sts)
Rnd 39 (blo): 1 sc in each sc. (24 sts)
Rnd 40: 1 sc in each sc. (24 sts)
Rnd 41: (2 sc in next sc, 1 sc in each of next 2 sc) 3 times, 2 sc in next sc, 1 sc in next 14 sc. (28 sts)
Rnds 42–49: 1 sc in each sc. (8 Rnds of 28 sts)

Rnd 50: 1 sc in each of next 5 sc, sc2tog in next 2 sc, 1 sc in each of next 2 sc, (sc2tog in next 2 sc) twice, 1 sc in each of next 2 sc, sc2tog in next 2 sc, 1 sc in each of next 11 sc. (24 sts)

Rnd 51: (1 sc in each of next 4 sc, sc2tog in next 2 sc) 4 times. (20 sts)

Rnd 52: (1 sc in each of next 3 sc, sc2tog in next 2 sc) 4 times. (16 sts)

Rnd 53: (sc2tog in next 2 sc) 3 times, 1 sc in each of next 4 sc, (sc2tog in next 2 sc) 3 times. (10 sts)
Stuff the body.

Rnd 54: (1 sc in each of next 3 sc, sc2tog in next 2 sc) twice. (8 sts)

Rnds 55–57: 1 sc in each sc. (3 Rnds of 8 sts)
Fasten off, adding a little more stuffing into the neck. Attach the head to the body, catching alternate stitches from the head and neck. Using col 2, add laces to the shoes.

ARMS (MAKE 2)

Using col 1, make a magic ring leaving 2¾" (7cm) tail (later to become the thumb).
Rnd 1: 4 sc into the ring and pull it closed. (4 sts)
Rnd 2: 2 sc in each of next 4 sc. (8 sts)
Rnds 3–4: 1 sc in each sc. (2 Rnds of 8 sts)
Rnd 5: sc2tog in next 2 sc, 1 sc in each of next 6 sc. (7 sts)
Rnd 6: sc2tog in next 2 sc, 1 sc in each of next 5 sc. (6 sts)
Rnds 7–14: 1 sc in each sc. (8 Rnds of 6 sts)
Rnd 15: sc2tog in next 2 sc, 1 sc in each of next 2 sc, 2 sc in next sc, 1 sc in next sc. (6 sts)
Rnd 16: 1 sc in each of next 3 sc, 1 hdc in each of next 3 sc.
Rnd 17: 1 sc in next sc, 2 sc in next sc, 1 sc in each of next 4 sts. (7 sts)
Rnds 18–25: 1 sc in each sc. (8 Rnds of 7 sts)
Stuff the arms lightly.
Insert the hook near the thumb position on the hand, out through the end of the hand and pull back the yarn tail. Insert the hook into the exact thumb position hole, pull the tail through to make a loop, ch 2, and then fasten off. Pull the end of the tail back through the same hole, leaving the thumb sticking out, and use the hook to hide the rest of the tail inside the arm.
Sew the arms to the body.

WIG CAP, HAIR, AND FACE

Using col 5, work Rnds 1–5 as for head. (30 sts)
Rnd 6: (1 sc in each of next 4 sc, 2 sc in next sc) 6 times. (36 sts)
Rnd 7: (1 sc in each of next 5 sc, 2 sc in next sc) 6 times. (42 sts)
Rnd 8: (1 sc in each of next 6 sc, 2 sc in next sc) 6 times. (48 sts)
Rnd 9: (1 sc in each of next 6 sc, sc2tog in next 2 sc) 6 times. (42 sts)
Rnds 10–11: 1 sc in each sc. (2 Rnds of 42 sts)

FRONT HAIR/BANGS

Rnd 12 (transition to rows): 1 sc in each of next 6 sc, turn. (6 sts)
Row 13: ch 1, 1 sc in each sc. (6 sts)
Fasten off wig cap, leaving a long tail for sewing.
Sew the cap at a slight angle to the back/top of the head, catching stitches around the edges of the cap, but not too tight as to distort the head shape.

Embroider a face onto your doll. For the nose, choose 4 sts in the center of the face and slip stitch around them, pulling the thread through with a needle.

Stitch a few strands of wool from the edge of the cap toward the back of the head to give a hairstyle as in the picture, or use your imagination to copy the hairstyle of your favorite soccer character.
For a short style, attach individual cut strands at random by inserting the hook under a sc, doubling a cut strand and catching a loop, pulling it partway through, and then insert the two loose ends through the loop, pulling tight.
Weave these randomly into the cap until it's covered. You can then cut and style the hair, but not too short otherwise the strands might pull through.

SHORTS

With the doll held upside down and facing away from you, join col 4 at the back of the doll's waist with ss to a loop from Rnd 40.
Rnds 1–2: 1 sc in each loop around waist. (24 sts)
Rnd 3: (1 sc in each of next 2 sc, 2 sc in next sc) 8 times. (32 sts)
Rnd 4: (1 sc in each of next 3 sc, 2 sc in next sc) 8 times. (40 sts)
Rnd 5–6: 1 sc in each sc. (2 rnds of 40 sts)

FIRST LEG

Skip 20 sts, then ss between the legs into 21st st from previous rnd. This divides the work into two, and you will now work each leg of the shorts separately.
Rnd 7: ch 3, 1 dc into ss just made, 1 dc in each of next 19 sc. (20 sts)
Rnd 8: ch 3, 1 dc in each dc, join with ss. (20 sts)
Fasten off. Weave the end to hide inside the leg.

SECOND LEG

With the doll still held upside down and facing away from you, rejoin col 4 with ss in st 40 from Rnd 6 (at inside leg).
Rnd 7: ch 3, 1 dc in each of next 19 sc, 1 dc in joining ss from 1st leg. (20 sts)
Rnd 8: ch 3, 1 dc in each of next 20 dc, join with ss. (20 sts)
Fasten off and weave the end inside the leg.

SHIRT

Using col 7, ch 17.
Row 1: 2 hdc in 3rd ch from hook and then 2 hdc in each ch to end, turn. (30 sts)
Row 2 (make armholes): ch 2, 1 hdc in next 5 hdc, ch 5, skip next 5 hdc, 1 hdc in each of next 10 hdc, ch 5, skip next 5 hdc, 1 hdc in each of next 5 hdc, turn. (30 sts)
Row 3: ch 2, 1 hdc in each of next 5 hdc, 5 hdc in ch-sp, 1 hdc in each of next 10 hdc, 5 hdc in ch-sp, 1 hdc in each of next 5 sc, turn. (30 sts)
Row 4–7: ch 2, 1 hdc in each of next 30 hdc, turn. (4 Rnds of 30 sts)
Row 8: ch 2, (1 hdc in each of next 9 hdc, 2 hdc in next hdc) twice, 1 hdc in each of next 10 hdc, turn. (32 sts)
Row 9: ch 2, (1 hdc in each of next 10 hdc, 2 hdc in next hdc) twice, 10 hdc, turn. (34 sts)
Row 10: ch 2, 1 hdc in each hdc. (34 sts)
Fasten off, leaving a long tail end.

SLEEVES (CROCHETED AROUND THE ARMHOLES)
Insert the hook in any st at the bottom of one of the armholes, ch 2 and begin working in rounds as follows:
Rnd 1: 1 hdc into same st, 13 hdc evenly around the armhole space (5 sts at top, 5 sts at bottom, 2 sts on each side). (14 sts).
Rnds 2–4: ch 2 (does not count as stitch),1 hdc into each hdc. (14 sts)
Fasten off and weave in ends.

SECOND SLEEVE
Insert the hook in any st at the bottom of the second armhole, pull through loop of yarn, make ch 2. Complete as for the first sleeve, working Rnds 1–4 above. Position the shirt on the doll, and use the tail end to neatly sew up the back from the bottom to the neck.

SOCCER BALL
Using col 7, make a magic ring.
Rnd 1: 6 sc into the ring and pull it closed. (6 sts)
Change to col 4.
Rnd 2: 2 sc in each of next 6 sc. (12 sts)
Rnd 3: (1 sc in next sc, 2 sc in next sc, 1 sc in each of next 2 sc, 2 sc in next sc) twice, 1 sc in next sc, 2 sc in next sc. (17 sts)
Rnd 4: 1 sc in each of next 2 sc, 2 sc in next sc, (1 sc in each of next 3 sc, 2 sc in next sc) 3 times, 1 sc in each of next 2 sc. (21 sts)
Rnd 5: (With col 4, 1 sc in each of next 3 sc, 2 sc in next sc, 1 sc in next sc, change to col 7, 1 sc in each of next 2 sc) 3 times. (24 sts)
Rnd 6: With col 4, 1 sc in each of next 6 sc, change to col 7, 1 sc in each of next 3 sc, change to col 4, 1 sc in next sc, 2 sc in next sc, 1 sc in each of next 3 sc, change to col 7, 1 sc in each of next 3 sc, change to col 4, 1 sc in each of next 5 sc, change to col 7, 1 sc in each of next 2 sc. (25 sts)
Rnd 7: With col 7, 1 sc in next sc, change to col 4, 1 sc in each of next 6 sc, change to col 7, 1 sc in each of next 2 sc, change to col 4, 1 sc in each of next 7dc, change to col 7, 1 sc in each of next 2 sc, change to col 4, 1 sc in each of next 6 sc, change to col 7, 1 sc in next sc. (25 sts)
Rnd 8: With col 7, 1 sc in next sc, change to col 4, 1 sc in each of next 12 sc, sc2tog in next 2 sc, 1 sc in each of next 10 sc. (24 sts)
Begin stuffing and continue in col 4.
Rnd 9: 1 sc in each of next 3 sc, (sc2tog in next 2 sc, 1 sc in each of next 6 sc) twice, sc2tog in next 2 sc, 1 sc in each of next 3 sc. (21 sts)
Rnd 10: 1 sc in each of next 2 sc, (sc2tog in next 2 sc, 1 sc in each of next 3 sc) 3 times, sc2tog in next 2 sc, 1 sc in each of next 2 sc. (17 sts)
Rnd 11: (sc2tog in next 2 sc, 1 sc in next sc, sc2tog in next 2 sc, 1 sc in each of next 2 sc) twice, sc2tog in next 2 sc, 1 sc in next sc. (12 sts)
Add more stuffing, if needed.
Change to col 7.
Rnd 12: (sc2tog in next 2 sc) 6 times. (6 sts)
Pull thread through remaining 6 sts, pull to close, and fasten off.
Darn in the ends.

TROPHY
Using col 8, make a magic ring.
Rnd 1: 6 sc into the ring and pull it closed. (6 sts)
Rnd 2: 2 sc in each of next 6 sc. (12 sts)
Rnd 3: (1 sc in next sc, 2 sc in next sc) 6 times. (18 sts)
Rnd 4 (flo): (1 sc in each of next 2 sc, 2 sc in next sc) 6 times, join with ss. (24 sts)
Fasten off.

Weave in the ends to the center so the loose ends come up the middle with the base sitting on protruding loops. Rejoin the yarn, with the loop through the center hole top. Join with ss, leaving the loose ends through the center of the ring, and continue to work around the loose ends as follows:

Rnd 5–7: ch 1, 6 sc around the center hole. (6 sts)
Rnd 8: 2 sc in each of next 3 sc. (12 sts)
Rnd 9: (1 sc in next sc, 2 sc in next sc) 6 times. (18 sts)
Rnd 10: (1 sc in each of next 2 sc, 2 sc in next sc) 6 times. (24 sts)
Rnd 11–20: 1 sc in each sc.
Fasten off neatly, leaving an 11¾" (29.8cm) tail to make handles.

MAKE HANDLES
Thread the tail inside the cup, and pull out to emerge one Rnd down the side of the cup (top of handle).
With the tail,, ch 12, fasten off, and pull through cup to form the handle. Secure to the side by hooking the tail around one more st, then across the inside bottom of the cup and out the opposite side. Secure again around a st, then ch 13 and secure the other end of the handle near the rim of the cup. Weave in loose ends. Use a needle and yarn to strengthen the handles, if you wish.

Giant mouse

This jumbo-sized amigurumi mouse is bigger than the mice
you'll find in mouse holes, but also much cuddlier!

NAME: **AMY KEMBER**
BIO: Amy is a technical writer
living in Ottawa, Canada. Her
interest in crochet began when
she discovered an amigurumi
book in a used bookstore. After
making a pig, she was instantly
hooked. Since 2010, Amy has
been designing and selling her
own amigurumi patterns on
Etsy.
www.etsy.com/shop/
AmysGurumis/

DIFFICULTY:
★ ★ ★ ☆ ☆

HOOK
F/5 (3.75mm)

YARN
In this project, we have used
Bernat Handicrafter Cotton. You
will need to use DK weight yarn in
your chosen colors.
Color: Body (3 balls)

NOTIONS
Yarn needle
Fiberfill
1 pair 9mm safety eyes
Pink & gray felt
Small pink button
Hot glue gun

MEASUREMENTS
13" (33cm) tall

APPROX TIME TAKEN
9 hours

GIANT MOUSE

HEAD
Using the hook, make a magic ring.
Rnd 1: 6 sc into ring and pull it closed. (6 sts)
Rnd 2: 2 sc in each sc. (12 sts)
Rnd 3: (1 sc in next sc, 2 sc in the next sc) 6 times.
(18 sts)
Rnd 4: (1 sc in each of next 2 sc, 2 sc in next sc) 6 times. (24 sts)
Rnd 5: (1 sc in each of next 3 sc, 2 sc in next sc) 6 times. (30 sts)
Rnd 6: (1 sc in each of next 4 sc, 2 sc in next sc) 6 times. (36 sts)
Rnd 7: (1 sc in each of next 5 sc, 2 sc in next sc) 6 times. (42 sts)
Rnds 8–12: 1 sc in each sc. (5 Rnds of 42 sts)
Rnd 13: ss In each sc. (42 sts)
Rnd 14: (1 sc in each of next 6 sc, 2 sc in next sc) 6 times. (48 sts)
Rnd 15: (1 sc in each of next 7 sc, 2 sc in next sc) 6 times. (54 sts)
Rnd 16: (1 sc in each of next 8 sc, 2 sc in next sc) 6 times. (60 sts)
Rnds 17–21: 1 sc in each sc. (5 Rnds of 60 sts)
Rnd 22: (1 sc in each of next 8 sc, sc2tog over next 2 sts) 6 times. (54 sts)
Rnd 23: (1 sc in each of next 7 sc, sc2tog over next 2 sts) 6 times. (48 sts)
Rnd 24: (1 sc in each of next 6 sc, sc2tog over next 2 sts) 6 times. (42 sts)
Rnd 25: (1 sc in each of next 5 sc, sc2tog over next 2 sts) 6 times. (36 sts)
Rnd 26: (1 sc in each of next 4 sc, sc2tog over next 2 sts) 6 times. (30 sts)
Rnd 27: (1 sc in each of next 3 sc, sc2tog over next 2 sts) 6 times. (24 sts)
Fasten off.

BODY
Make a magic ring.
Rnd 1: 6 sc into ring and pull it closed. (6 sts)
Rnd 2: 2 sc in each sc. (12 sts)
Rnd 3: (1 sc in next sc, 2 sc in next sc) 6 times.
(18 sts)
Rnd 4: (1 sc in each of next 2 sc, 2 sc in next sc) 6 times. (24 sts)
Rnd 5: (1 sc in each of next 3 sc, 2 sc in next sc) 6 times. (30 sts)

Rnd 6: (1 sc in each of next 4 sc, 2 sc in next sc) 6 times. (36 sts)
Rnd 7: (1 sc in each of next 5 sc, 2 sc in next sc) 6 times. (42 sts)
Rnd 8: (1 sc in each of next 6 sc, 2 sc in next sc) 6 times. (48 sts)
Rnd 9: (1 sc in each of next 7 sc, 2 sc in next sc) 6 times. (54 sts)
Rnds 10–12: 1 sc in each sc. (3 Rnds of 54 sts)
Rnd 13: (1 sc in each of next 7 sc, sc2tog over next 2 sts) 6 times. (48 sts)
Rnds 14–17: sc in each sc. (4 Rnds of 48 sts)
Rnd 18: (1 sc in each of next 6 sc, sc2tog over next 2 sts) 6 times. (42 sts)
Rnds 19–20: 1 sc in each sc. (2 Rnds of 42 sts)
Rnd 21: (1 sc in each of next 5 sc, sc2tog over next 2 sts) 6 times. (36 sts)
Rnd 22: (1 sc In each of next 4 sc, sc2tog over next 2 sts) 6 times. (30 sts)
Rnds 23–25: 1 sc in each sc. (3 Rnds of 30 sts)
Fasten off.

EARS (MAKE 2)

Make a magic ring.
Rnd 1: 6 sc into ring and pull it closed. (6 sts)
Rnd 2: 2 sc in each sc. (12 sts)
Rnd 3: (1 sc in next sc, 2 sc in next sc) 6 times. (18 sts)
Rnd 4: (1 sc in each of the next 2 sc, 2 sc in next sc) 6 times. (24 sts)
Rnds 5–8: 1 sc in each sc. (4 Rnds of 24 sts)
Rnd 9: (1 sc in each of next 2 sc, sc2tog over next 2 sts) 6 times. (18 sts)
Rnd 10: (1 sc in next sc, sc2tog over next 2 sts) 6 times. (12 sts)
Fasten off.

ARMS (MAKE 2)

Make a magic ring.
Rnd 1: 6 sc into ring and pull it closed. (6 sts)
Rnd 2: 2 sc in each sc. (12 sts)
Rnd 3: (1 sc in next sc, 2 sc in next sc) 6 times. (18 sts)
Rnds 4–5: 1 sc in each sc. (2 Rnds of 18 sts)
Rnd 6: (1 sc in next sc, sc2tog over next 2 sts) 6 times. (12 sts)
Rnds 7–12: 1 sc in each sc. (6 Rnds of 12 sts)
Rnd 13: (sc2tog over next 2 sts) 6 times. (6 sts)
Fasten off.

LEGS (MAKE 2)

Make a magic ring.
Rnd 1: 6 sc into ring and pull it closed. (6 sts)
Rnd 2: 2 sc in each sc. (12 sts)
Rnd 3: (1 sc in next sc, 2 sc in next sc) 6 times. (18 sts)
Rnd 4: (1 sc in each of next 2 sc, 2 sc in next sc) 6 times. (24 sts)
Rnds 5–7: 1 sc in each sc. (3 Rnds of 24 sts)
Rnd 8: (1 sc in each of next 2 sc, sc2tog over next 2 sts) 6 times. (18 sts)

Rnd 9: (1 sc in next sc, sc2tog over next 2 sts) 6 times. (12 sts)
Rnds 10–15: 1 sc in each sc. (6 Rnds of 12 sts)
Fasten off.

TAIL

Ch 31.
1 sc into 2nd ch from hook, 1 sc into each ch to end (30 sts)
Fasten off.

FINISHING

ASSEMBLE THE FACE

Insert the safety eyes between Rnd 13 and Rnd 14 of the head, and position them approximately eight stitches apart. Stuff the head firmly.
Cut out a gray felt muzzle as shown in the picture below. Sew a pink button nose in the center of the muzzle using a yarn needle and yarn. Referring to the photograph, position the muzzle and nose between the eyes. Glue the muzzle and nose to the mouse's face using a hot glue gun.

ASSEMBLE THE BODY

Stuff the body, arms, and legs.
Sew the body to the head—note there is one extra decrease Rnd on the head than on the body, so the last Rnd of the body (Rnd 26) should be sewn around the second to last Rnd on the head (Rnd 27).
Sew the arms to the body between Rnd 25 and Rnd 26, positioning them six stitches apart on the front.
Sew the legs to the body between Rnd 8 and Rnd 9, positioning them two stitches apart in the front.
Cut out two pink felt circles for the ears. Glue felt to each crocheted ear using a hot glue gun. Sew the ears to the head between Rnd 10 and Rnd 14.
Sew the tail to the body between Rnd 10 and Rnd 11.

Cup of bear

- -

Teatime is the sweetest time of the day; what better way to enjoy it than in the company of this adorable bear in a cup? Add some cookies and enjoy!

NAME:

ANNERIS KONDRATAS

BIO: Anneris is an illustrator, designer, crochet artist, and above all, mother. Everything started as a hobby, writing a blog about food characters and creatures that she called Amigurumi Food. www.amigurumifood.com/

DIFFICULTY:

★ ★ ★ ★ ☆

HOOKS

C/2 or D/2 (3mm), main hook
B/1 (2.25mm), for bear's muzzle

YARN

For this project, we have used Red Heart Super Saver and Lion Brand. You will need a DK weight yarn in your chosen colors.

Cup and Bear:

Color 1: Main cup color (1 ball)
Color 2: Main cup accent color (scrap yarn)
Color 3: Secondary cup accent color (scrap yarn)
Color 4: Liquid in cup (1 ball)
Color 5: Tea bag tag (scrap yarn)
Color 6: Bear body (1 ball)

Sandwich cookies:

Color 1: Topping (scrap yarn)
Color 2: Body (1 ball)
Color 3: Filling (scrap yarn)

NOTIONS

Beige & pink embroidery thread
3 or more pairs 4mm safety eyes
Green & light pink felt

MEASUREMENTS

Cup and bear: 6¼" x 7" (15.9 x 17.8cm)
Cookies: 2" (5.1cm) diameter

APPROX TIME TAKEN

4 hours

SPECIAL STITCHES

Reverse single crochet (rsc) (see page 159)
3dc popcorn stitch (3dc-pop) (see page 159)

CUP OF BEAR

CUP

Using col 1, make a magic ring.

Rnd 1 (RS): 6 sc in magic ring, pull ring tight to close. (6 sts)

Rnd 2: 2 sc in each st around. (12 sts)

Rnd 3: (1 sc in next st, 2 sc in next st) 6 times. (18 sts)

Rnd 4: (1 sc in next 2 sts, 2 sc in next st) 6 times. (24 sts)

Rnd 5: (1 sc in next 3 sts, 2 sc in next st) 6 times. (30 sts)

Rnd 6: (1 sc in next 4 sts, 2 sc in next st) 6 times. (36 sts)

Rnd 7: (1 sc in next 5 sts, 2 sc in next st) 6 times. (42 sts)

Rnd 8 (blo): 1 sc in each st around. (42 sts)

Rnd 9: 1 sc in each st around. (42 sts)

Rnd 10: (1 sc in next 5 sts, sc2tog) 6 times. (36 sts)

Rnd 11: (1 sc in next 3 sts, 2 sc in next st) 9 times. (45 sts)

Rnd 12: (1 sc in next 4 sts, 2 sc in next st) 9 times. (54 sts)

Rnd 13: (1 sc in next 5 sts, 2 sc in next st) 9 times. (63 sts)

Rnd 14: (1 sc in next 6 sts, 2 sc in next st) 9 times. (72 sts)

Rnds 15–20: 1 sc in each st around. (6 Rnds of 72 sts)
Fix safety eyes between Rnds 19 and 20.

Note: For the next 3 Rnds, always change col during the last yo of the last sc before the col change, which leaves the ring on the hook in the new col ready for the next st.

Rnd 21: Using col 1, 1 sc in next 2 sts, in col 2, 1 sc in next st, in col 1, 1 sc in next 2 sts, in col 3, 1 sc in next st, in col 1, 1 sc in next 2 sts, *in col 2, 1 sc in next st, in col 1, 1 sc in next 2

sts, in col 3, 1 sc in next st, in col 1, 1 sc in next 2 sts; rep from * another 9 times, in col 2, 1 sc in next st, in col 1, 1 sc in next 2 sts, in col 3, 1 sc in next st. (66 sts)

Rnds 22–23: in col 1, 1 sc in next st, in col 2, 1 sc in next 3 sts, in col 1, 1 sc in next 3 sts, * in col 2, 1 sc in next 3 sts, in col 1, 1 sc in next 3 sts; rep from * another 9 times, in col 2, 1 sc in next 3 sts, in col 1, 1 sc in next 2 sts. (2 rnds of 66 sts)

Rnd 24: in col 1 1 sc in each st around. (66 sts)

Rnd 25: rdc in each st around. ss in first st, cut yarn and fasten off.

LIQUID IN CUP

Using col 4, make a magic ring.

Rnd 1 (RS): 6 sc in magic ring, pull ring tight to close. (6 sts)

Rnd 2: 2 sc in each st around. (12 sts)

Rnd 3: (1 sc in next st, 2 sc in next st) 6 times. (18 sts)

Rnd 4: (1 sc in next 2 sts, 2 sc in next st) 6 times. (24 sts)

Rnd 5: (1 sc in next 3 sts, 2 sc in next st) 6 times. (30 sts)

Rnd 6: (1 sc in next 4 sts, 2 sc in next st) 6 times. (36 sts)

Rnd 7: (1 sc in next 5 sts, 2 sc in next st) 6 times. (42 sts)

Rnd 8: (1 sc in next 6 sts, 2 sc in next st) 6 times. (48 sts)

Rnd 9: (1 sc in next 7 sts, 2 sc in next st) 6 times. (54 sts)

Rnd 10: (1 sc in next 8 sts, 2 sc in next st) 6 times. (60 sts)

Rnd 11: (1 sc in next 9 sts, 2 sc in next st) 6 times. (66 sts)

Rnd 12: (1 sc in next 10 sts, 2 sc in next st) 6 times. (72 sts)
ss in next st, fasten off, and leave a long tail for sewing.

CUP HANDLE

Using col 1, make a magic ring.
Rnd 1 (RS): 6 sc in magic ring, pull ring tight to close. (6 sts)
Rnds 2–14: 1 sc in each st around. (13 Rnds of 6 sts)
ss in next st, fasten off, and leave a long tail for sewing.
No stuffing is needed for the handle.

SAUCER

Using col 1, make a magic ring.
Rnd 1 (RS): 6 sc in magic ring, pull ring tight to close. (6 sts)
Rnds 2–11: Work as given for Liquid in Cup Rnds 2–11.
Rnd 12–13: 1 sc in each st around. (2 Rnds of 66 sts)
Rnd 14: rsc in each sc. (66 sts)
ss in next st, cut yarn and fasten off.

TEA BAG TAG

Using col 5, ch 5.
Row 1 (RS): 1 sc in second ch from hook, 1 sc in next 4 sts, turn. (4 sts)
Row 2: ch 1 (not counted as a st), 1 sc in next 4 sts, turn.
Row 3: ch 1 (not counted as a st), 1 sc in next 4 sts, do not turn, ch 1 then work a sc border all around the edge, working 2 sc in each corner.
ss in first sc, fasten off and leave a long tail for sewing. Cut the shape of a small leaf from felt and hot glue it to the tag.

Set the cup pieces aside. You will assemble the entire figure once you've made the remaining bear and cookie pieces.

BEAR HEAD & BODY

Using col 6, make a magic ring.
Rnd 1 (RS): 6 sc in magic ring, pull ring tight to close. (6 sts)
Rnd 2: 2 sc in each st around. (12 sts)
Rnd 3: (1 sc in next st, 2 sc in next st) 6 times. (18 sts)
Rnd 4: (1 sc in next 2 sts, 2 sc in next st) 6 times. (24 sts)
Rnd 5: (1 sc in next 3 sts, 2 sc in next st) 6 times. (30 sts)
Rnds 6–9: 1 sc in each st around. (4 Rnds of 30 sts)
Fix safety eyes along Rnd 7, approximately 3 sts apart.
Rnd 10: (1 sc in next 3 sts, sc2tog) 6 times. (24 sts)
Rnd 11: (1 sc in next 2 sts, sc2tog) 6 times. (18 sts)
Rnd 12: 1 sc in each st in each sc. (18 sts)
Rnd 13: (1 sc in next 2 sts, 2 sc in next st) 6 times. (24 sts)
Rnd 14: (1 sc in next 3 sts, 2 sc in next st) 6 times. (30 sts)
Rnd 15: 1 sc in each sc. (30 sts)
ss in next st, fasten off and leave a long tail for sewing.

Fill the bear firmly with stuffing.
Embroider the cheeks with pink embroidery thread by making two horizontal backstitches with doubled thread.

ARMS (MAKE 2)

Using col 6, make a magic ring.
Rnd 1 (RS): 6 sc in magic ring, pull ring tight to close. (6 sts)
Rnd 2: (1 sc in next st, 2 sc in next st) 3 times. (9 sts)
Rnd 3: 3dc-pop in next st, 1 sc in next 8 sts. (9 sts)
Rnd 4–10: 1 sc in each st around. (7 rnds of 9 sts)
ss in next st, fasten off, and leave a long tail for sewing. Insert a small amount of stuffing inside the arms, so that they bend easily.

EARS (MAKE 2)
Using col 6, make a magic ring.
Rnd 1 (RS): 6 sc in magic ring, pull ring tight to close.
(6 sts)
Rnd 2: (1 sc in next st, 2 sc in next st) 3 times. (9 sts)
Rnd 3: 1 sc in each sc. (9 sts)
ss in next st, fasten off and leave a long tail for sewing.

FEET (MAKE 2)
Using col 6, make a magic ring.
Rnd 1 (RS): 6 sc in magic ring, pull ring tight to close.
(6 sts)
Rnd 2: (1 sc in next st, 2 sc in next st) 3 times. (9 sts)
Rnds 3–4: 1 sc in each sc. (2 Rnds of 9 sts)
ss in next st, fasten off, and leave a long tail for sewing.

BACK PAWS
Working with beige embroidery thread:
First, embroider a rectangular shape (for the large
metacarpal pad), then fill the shape with vertical
backstitches. Do not cut the thread yet.
Now, embroider four smaller digital pads made up of
three backstitches each.

MUZZLE
Using the small hook and beige embroidery thread, make
a magic ring.
Rnd 1 (RS): 6 sc in magic ring, pull ring tight to close.
(6 sts)
Rnd 2: 2 sc in each st around. (12 sts)
Rnds 3–4: 1 sc in each sc. (2 Rnds of 12 sts)
ss in next st, fasten off, and leave a long tail for sewing.

Set the bear pieces aside. You will assemble the entire
figure once you've made the remaining cookie pieces.

SANDWICH COOKIE
(Make at least 1)
Using col 1, make a magic ring.
Rnd 1 (RS): 6 sc in magic ring, pull ring tight to close. (6 sts)
Rnd 2: 2 sc in each st around, changing to col 2 on last yo of
last sc. (12 sts)
Rnd 3: ss loosely in each st around. (12 sts)

Rnd 4 (blo): (1 sc in next st, 2 sc in next st) 6 times.
(18 sts)
Rnd 5: (1 sc in next 2 sts, 2 sc in next st) 6 times. (24 sts)
Fix safety eyes between Rnds 4 and 5.
Rnd 6 (blo): 1 sc in each st around, changing to col 3 on
last yo of last sc. (24 sts)
Rnd 7: In col 3, 1 sc in each st around, changing
to col 2 on last yo of last sc. (24 sts)
Rnd 8 (blo): 1 sc in each st around. (24 sts)
Rnd 9: 1 sc in each st around. (24 sts)
Rnd 10: (1 sc in next 2 sts, sc2tog) 6 times. (18 sts)
Stuff the cookie.
Rnd 11: (1 sc in next st, sc2tog) 6 times. (12 sts)
Rnd 12: (sc2tog) 6 times. (6 sts)
ss in next st and fasten off.
Embroider the mouth with white thread by making
two diagonal backstitches.

FINISHING

FINISH AND ATTACH THE BEAR
Embroider a mouth on the muzzle with brown thread by
making one vertical backstitch and an upside down V.
Embroider the nose with pink thread by making a triangle
and then filling it with backstitches.
Sew the arms to the bear. Place one cookie between the
front paws. Attach the bear to the liquid in cup section as
shown in the pictures.
Fill the back paws with a small amount of stuffing, and
sew them to the liquid in cup section as shown in the
main project photo on page 136.

ASSEMBLE THE CUP
Sew the tea bag tag to the liquid in cup piece.
Sew the handle to the right side of the cup, then sew the
cup to the saucer.
Fill the cup with fiberfill.
Sew the liquid in cup piece (with the bear and tea bag tag
already sewn to it) onto the top of the cup.
Cut a small half circle of light pink felt to create a mouth
and center, and hot glue it slightly below the safety eyes.
Embroider the cup cheeks with beige embroidery thread
by making two horizontal backstitches with doubled
thread.

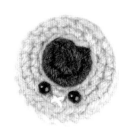

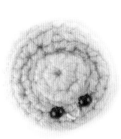

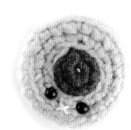

Halloween rat

With realistic shaping and scary red eyes, this creepy-cute rat is
a great addition to any Halloween costume or decoration.

NAME: **KATI GÁLUSZ**

BIO: Kati is an amigurumi designer from Hungary. She loves to create patterns for realistic animals, and for her favorite movie and TV characters. www.ravelry.com/designers/kati-galusz

DIFFICULTY:
★ ★ ★ ☆ ☆

HOOK
C/2 or D/3 (3mm)

YARN
In this project, we have used Hayfield Bonus DK. You will need a DK weight yarn in your chosen colors.
Color 1: Body (1 ball)
Color 2: Ears, paws, and tail (1 ball)

NOTIONS
Stitch markers
1 pair 7.5mm red safety eyes
Fiberfill
Yarn needle

MEASUREMENTS
5½"–6" (14–15.2cm) long (without tail), 2½"–3" (6.4–7.6cm) tall

APPROX TIME TAKEN
4 hours

HALLOWEEN RAT

HEAD AND BODY

Using col 1, make a magic ring
Rnd 1 (RS): 6 sc in magic ring, pull ring tight to close. (6 sts)
Rnd 2: (1 sc in next st, 2 sc in next st, 1 sc in next st) twice. (8 sts)
Rnd 3: (2 sc in next st, 1 sc in next 3 sts) twice. (10 sts)
Rnd 4: (1 sc in next 2 sts, 2 sc in next st, 1 sc in next 2 sts) twice. (12 sts)
Rnd 5: (2 sc in next st, 1 sc in next 5 sts) twice. (14 sts)
Rnd 6: (1 sc in next 3 sts, 2 sc in next st, 1 sc in next 3 sts) twice. (16 sts)
Rnd 7: 1 sc in each st around. (16 sts)

Attach a removable stitch marker into the 3rd st of the Rnd you just completed; this will help with the placement of the eyes.

Rnd 8: (2 sc in next st, 1 sc in next 7 sts) twice. (18 sts)
Rnd 9: 1 sc in each st around. (18 sts)
Rnd 10: (1 sc in next 4 sts, 2 sc in next st, 1 sc in next 4 sts) twice. (20 sts)
Rnd 11: 1 sc in next 13 sts, 2 sc in next st, 1 sc in next 2 sts, 2 sc in next st, 1 sc in next 3 sts. (22 sts)
Rnd 12: 1 sc in next 13 sts, (2 sc in next st, 1 sc in next 2 sts) 3 times. (25 sts)
Rnd 13: 1 sc in next 4 sts, sc2tog, 1 sc in next 10 sts, 2 sc in next st, 1 sc in next 2 sts, 2 sc in next st, 1 sc in next 5 sts. (26 sts)
Rnd 14: 1 sc in next 4 sts, sc2tog, 1 sc in next 9 sts, 2 sc in next st, 1 sc in next 3 sts, 2 sc in next st, 1 sc in next 6 sts. (27 sts)
Rnd 15: 1 sc in next 4 sts, sc2tog, 1 sc in next 11 sts, 2 sc in next st, 1 sc in next 9 sts. (27 sts)
Rnds 16–17: 1 sc in each st around. (2 Rnds of 27 sts)
Rnd 18: 1 sc in next 4 sts, 2 sc in next st, 1 sc in next 22 sts. (28 sts)
Rnd 19: 1 sc in each st around. (28 sts)

Attach the safety eyes between Rnds 7 and 8, about six stitches apart (the stitch marker shows the top of the head). Remove the marker, and stuff the head.

Rnd 20: 1 sc in next 4 sts, 2 sc in next st, 1 sc in next 2 sts, 2 sc in next st, 1 sc in next 20 sts. (30 sts)
Rnd 21: 1 sc in each st around. (30 sts)
Rnd 22: 1 sc in next 5 sts, 2 sc in next st, 1 sc in next 2 sts, 2 sc in next st, 1 sc in next 21 sts. (32 sts)
Rnd 23: 1 sc in each st around. (32 sts)
Rnd 24: 1 sc in next 6 sts, 2 sc in next st, 1 sc in next 2 sts, 2 sc in next st, 1 sc in next 22 sts (34 sts)
Rnd 25: 1 sc in each st around. (34 sts)
Rnd 26: 1 sc in next 8 sts, 2 sc in next st, 1 sc in next 2 sts, 2 sc in next st, 1 sc in next 22 sts (36 sts)
Rnds 27–30: 1 sc in each st around. (4 Rnds of 36 sts)
Rnd 31: 1 sc in next 8 sts, sc2tog, 1 sc in next 3 sts, sc2tog, 1 sc in next 21 sts. (34 sts)
Rnd 32: 1 sc in each st around. (34 sts)
Rnd 33: 1 sc in next 7 sts, sc2tog, 1 sc in next 3 sts, sc2tog, 1 sc in next 20 sts. (32 sts)
Rnd 34: 1 sc in each st around. (32 sts)

Rnd 35: (1 sc in next 3 sts, sc2tog, 1 sc in next 3 sts) 4 times. (28 sts)
Rnd 36: 1 sc in each st around. (28 sts)
Rnd 37: (sc2tog, 1 sc in next 5 sts) 4 times. (24 sts)
Rnd 38: (1 sc in next 2 sts, sc2tog, 1 sc in next 2 sts) 4 times. (20 sts)
Rnd 39: (sc2tog, 1 sc in next 3 sts) 4 times. (16 sts)
Start stuffing the rat, then add some more filling after Rnd 40.
Rnd 40: (1 sc in next st, sc2tog, 1 sc in next st) 4 times. (12 sts)
Rnd 41: (sc2tog) 6 times. (6 sts)
Change to col 2.
Rnds 42–43: 1 sc in each st around. (2 Rnds of 6 sts)
Rnd 44: sc2tog, 1 sc in next 4 sts. (5 sts)

From here on, you will work even Rnds until the tail tip. Using a stitch marker is difficult in such short rounds, so it is easier to count the stitches rather than the Rnds. Or you can stop counting at all and just crochet around until the tail looks long enough.

Rnds 45–69: 1 sc in each st around (5 sts x 25 Rnds = 125 sts altogether). ss in next st, fasten off and use the yarn end to sew the tail tip closed. (25 Rnds of 5 sts)

FRONT LEGS (MAKE 2)

Using col 2, make a magic ring.
Rnd 1 (RS): 6 sc in magic ring, pull ring tight to close. (6 sts)
Rnd 2: 1 sc in next 3 sts, change to col 1, 1 sc in next 3 sts.
Rnd 3: 1 sc in next 4 sts, 2 sc in next st, 1 sc in next st. (7 sts)
Rnd 4: 1 sc in next 5 sts, 2 sc in next st, 1 sc in next st. (8 sts)
Rnd 5: 1 sc in next 2 sts, sc2tog, 1 sc in next 2 sts, 2 sc in next st, 1 sc in next st. (8 sts)
Rnd 6: 1 sc in each st around. (8 sts)
ss in next st, fasten off, leaving a long yarn end.

The col 2 stitches in Rnd 2 show the top of the paws. Stuff the legs and sew them to the body. The front edge should be roughly at Rnd 14.

REAR FEET (MAKE 2)

Using col 2, make a magic ring.
Rnd 1 (RS): 5 sc in magic ring, pull ring tight to close. (5 sts)
Rnds 2–7: 1 sc in each st around. (6 Rnds of 5 sts)
ss in next st and fasten off, leaving a long yarn end.

Pin the foot to the body at ground level with the open end about 6 Rnds in front of the tail. Sew the open end to the body (closing the foot in the process). Then, make a few stitches between the body and foot about halfway forward to anchor them in the right position.

EARS (MAKE 2)

Using col 2, ch 5.
1 sc in 4th ch from hook, ch 2, sl st in next ch.
Fasten off, leaving a long yarn end. Sew the ears to the top of the head, 3 Rnds behind the eyes and about three stitches apart.

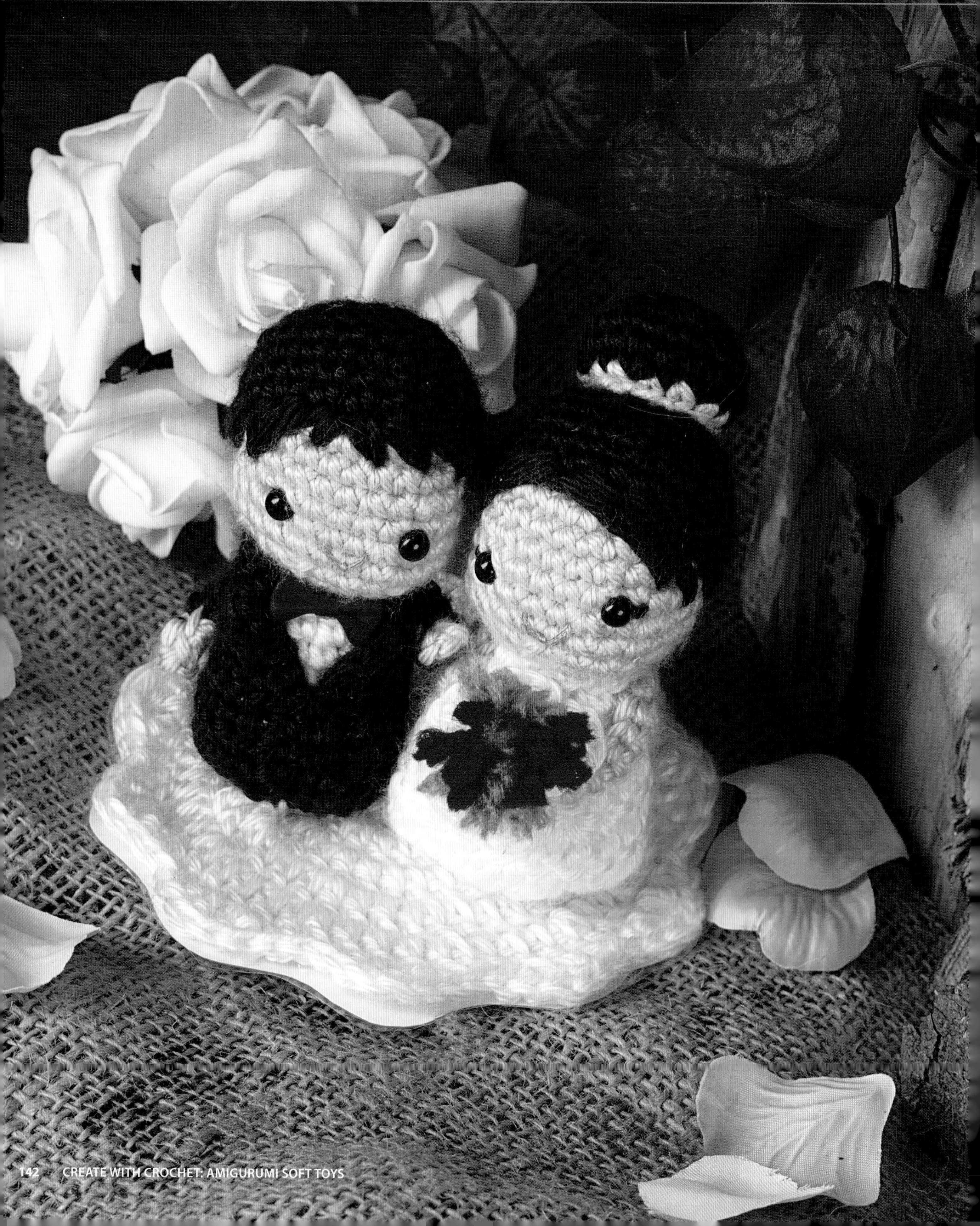

Wedding dolls

This darling bride and groom are easily customizable and make perfect handmade wedding gifts, can be used as decoration, or could even be a cake topper!

NAME: **JASMIN WANG**

BIO: Jasmin is an artist and crafter who enjoys illustrating, painting, sewing, origami, and of course, crocheting! She loves bringing figures, ideas, and other concepts to life through the art of crochet. Jasmin also enjoys spending time with her husband in their American Pacific Northwest home.
www.etsy.com/shop/Sylemn,
www.facebook.com/SweetSofties

DIFFICULTY:
★ ★ ★ ☆ ☆

HOOK
D/3 (3.25mm)

YARN
For this project, we have used Caron Simply Soft. You will need medium weight yarn in your chosen colors.
Color 1: Skin (1 ball)
Color 2: Hair (1 ball)
Color 3: Dress (1 ball)
Color 4: Suit (1 Ball)
Color 5: Dark flowers (scrap yarn)
Color 6: Light flowers (scrap yarn)

NOTIONS
2 pairs 6mm safety eyes
Embroidery thread
Scissors
Stitch marker (optional)
Fiberfill
Beads/pellets for weighted stuffing in the body
Small, decorative craft bow
Yarn & embroidery needle
Hot glue gun (optional)

MEASUREMENTS
3 ¾" (9.5cm) tall, 5" (12.7cm) diameter

APPROX TIME TAKEN
6 hours

BRIDE

HEAD
Using col 1, make a magic ring.
Rnd 1 (RS): ch 1, 6 sc in magic ring, join with ss. (6 sts)
Rnd 2: ch 1, 2 sc in each st around, join with ss. (12 sts)
Rnd 3: ch 1, (1 sc in next st, 2 sc in next st) 6 times, ss to first ch. (18 sts)
Rnd 4: ch 1, (1 sc in next 2 sts, 2 sc in next st) 6 times, ss to first ch. (24 sts)
Rnds 5–9: ch 1, 1 sc in each st around, ss to first ch. (5 Rnds of 24 sts)
Rnd 10: ch 1, (1 sc in next 2 sts, sc2tog) 6 times, ss to first ch. (18 sts)
Rnd 11: ch 1, (1 sc in next st, sc2tog) 6 times, ss to first ch. (12 sts)
Fasten off. Fix the safety eyes between Rnds 7 and 8, 5 sts apart. Stuff head firmly, taking care not to overstretch the stitches.

HAIR CAP
Using col 2, make a magic ring.
Rnd 1: ch 1, 6 sc in magic ring, join with ss. (6 sts)
Rnd 2: ch 1, 2 sc in each st around, ss to first ch. (12 sts)
Rnd 3: ch 1, (1 sc in next st, 2 sc in next st) 6 times, ss to first ch. (18 sts)
Rnd 4: ch 1, (1 sc in next 2 sts, 2 sc in next st) 6 times, ss to first ch. (24 sts)
Rnds 5–8: ch 1, 1 sc in each st around, ss to first ch. (4 Rnds of 24 sts)
Fasten off, leaving a long tail for attaching to the head later. If you are making Bride's Hair Option #2, do not fasten off and instead skip to that section.

BRIDE'S HAIR OPTION #1: BUN
Using col 2, make a magic ring.
Rnd 1: ch 1, 6 sc in magic ring, ss to first ch. (6 sts)
Rnd 2: ch 1, 2 sc in each st around, ss to first ch. (12 sts)
Rnd 3: ch 1, (1 sc in next st, 2 sc in next st) 6 times, ss to first ch. (18 sts)
Rnds 4–5: ch 1, 1 sc in each st around, ss to first ch. (3 Rnds of 18 sts)
Change to col 3 to create a contrasting hair tie/ribbon.
Rnd 6: ch 1, (1 sc in next st, sc2tog) 6 times, ss to first ch. (12 sts)
Fasten off, making sure to leave a long tail for attaching to the hair cap later.

BRIDE'S HAIR OPTION #2: CURLY PONYTAIL
Using col 2, follow instructions as given for the hair cap but do not fasten off at end. Next, make ch 15, *1 sc in 2nd ch from hook, 1 sc in each remaining ch (14 sts)*, ss into the next st along hair cap, make 18ch, 1 sc in 2nd ch from hook, 1 sc in each remaining ch (17 sts), ss into the next st along the hair cap, make ch 1, rep from * to *, ss in next st along the hair cap.

Fasten off, leaving a long tail for attaching this hair cap and curly ponytail to the head later.

BRIDE'S HAIR OPTION #3: DOWN AND LOOSE
Using col 2, follow instructions as given for the hair cap and sew to head.
Cut approximately 30 strands of col 2 to a little more than double the desired hair length. For example, if you would like your doll's hair to be 4" (10.2cm) from root to tip, cut 8" (20.3cm) strands.
Using a yarn needle threaded with a long strand of col 2, insert the needle from inside the head to the outside spot where the hairline begins.
Hold a bundle of three to five strands of yarn at a time, fold them in half, and then position the folded strands at the hairline spot.
Slip the needle back into the same stitch, pulling the bundle onto the head with a tight stitch.
Continue attaching small bundles of three to five strands until your doll has a full head of hair.

Pattern Gallery

BRIDE'S ARMS (MAKE 2)
Using col 1, ch8.
Row 1: 1 sc in 2nd ch from hook, 1 sc in each remaining ch. (7 sts)
Fasten off, leaving a long tail for attaching.

BRIDE'S BODY
Using col 3, make a magic ring.
Rnd 1: ch 1, 6 sc in magic ring, join with ss. (6 sts)
Rnd 2: ch 1, 2 sc in each st around, ss to first ch. (12 sts)
Rnd 3: ch 1, (1 sc in next st, 2 sc in next st) 6 times, ss to first ch. (18 sts)
Rnd 4 (blo): ch 1, 1 sc in each st around, ss to first ch. (18 sts)
Rnds 5–6: ch 1, 1 sc in each st around, ss to first ch. (2 Rnds of 18 sts)
Rnd 7: ch 1, (1 sc in next 7 sts, sc2tog) twice, ss to first ch. (16 sts)
Rnd 8: ch 1, 1 sc in each st around, ss to first ch. (16 sts)
Rnd 9: ch 1, (1 sc in next 6 sts, sc2tog) twice, ss to first ch. (14 sts)
Rnd 10: ch 1, 1 sc in each st around, ss to first ch. (14 sts)
Rnd 11: ch 1, (1 sc in next 5 sts, sc2tog) twice, ss to first ch. (12 sts)
Fasten off, leaving a long tail for attaching to the head later.

Note: When stuffing the body, add some beads/pellets to the bottom to give the amigurumi some weight and stability. Then, stuff the rest of the body with fiberfill.

BRIDE'S DRESS
The dress is a continuation of the body.
Using col 3, join yarn to the starting st on the backside of the bride's body, at Rnd 8.
Rnd 1 (RS): ch 1, 1 sc in each st around, join with ss. (16 sts)
Rnd 2: 3 ch (does not count as a st), 1 dc in same st at base of 3 ch, 1 dc in each st around, ss to top of first dc (missing the 3 ch). (16 sts)
Rnd 3: 3 ch, (does not count as a st), (1 dc in next 3 sts, 2 dc in next st) 4 times, ss to top of first dc (missing the 3 ch). (20 sts)
Rnd 4: Ch 3, (does not count as a st), (1 dc in next 4 sts, 2 dc in next st) 4 times, ss to top of first dc (missing the 3 ch). (24 sts)
Now, make a scalloped edge to the dress.
Rnd 5: ch 1 (not counted as a st), (1 sc in next st, (1 hdc, 1 sc) in next st, (1 sc, 1 hdc) in next st, 1 sc in next st) 6 times, ss to first ch. (36 sts)
Fasten off and weave in ends.

FLOWER BOUQUET
Using col 3, make a magic ring.
Rnd 1: ch 1, 5 sc in magic ring, join with ss. (5 sts)
Rnd 2: Ch 2, *(2 dc, ch 1, 1 sc) in next st, ch 1; rep from * 4 more times, ss to top of beginning 2 ch.
Fasten off, leaving a long tail for attaching.

BOUQUET ASSEMBLY:
Cut some short pieces of cols 5 and 6. Line them up. Using a long piece of col 3, tie them tightly together in the middle.
Pull the two ends of col 3 through the center of the crocheted bouquet piece. Tie the ends tightly to

secure the "flowers." Trim the tip of the flowers with scissors.
Hold the bouquet in a cone shape. With a yarn needle on the flower bouquet tail, insert a couple of stitches through the tip of the cone to keep it in that shape. Fasten off, leaving a long tail for attaching to the bride later.

GROOM

HEAD
Complete as for Bride's head.

HAIR CAP
Complete as for Bride's hair cap.

GROOM'S ARMS (MAKE 2)
Using col 4, ch5, change to col 1, ch3.
Row 1: 1 sc in 2nd ch from hook, 1 sc in next ch changing to col 4 on last yo, 1 sc in each remaining ch. (7 sts)
Fasten off, leaving a long tail for attaching.

GROOM'S BODY
Using col 4, make a magic ring.
Rnd 1: ch 1, 6 sc in magic ring, join with ss. (6 sts)
Rnd 2: ch 1, 2 sc in each st around, ss to first ch. (12 sts)
Rnd 3: ch 1, (1 sc in next st, 2 sc in next st) 6 times, ss to first ch. (18 sts)
Rnd 4: ch 1, 1 scblo in each st around, ss to first ch. (18 sts)
Rnd 5: ch 1, 1 sc in each st around, ss to first ch. (18 sts)
Rnd 6: ch 1, (1 sc in next st, sc2tog) 6 times, ss to first ch changing to col 3 on yo of ss. (12 sts)
Rnds 7–12: ch 1, 1 sc in each st around, ss to first ch. (12 sts)
Fasten off, leaving a long tail for attaching to the head later.

Note: When stuffing the body, add some beads/pellets to the bottom to give the amigurumi some weight and stability. Then, stuff the rest of the body with fiberfill.

GROOM'S SUIT JACKET
Using col 4, ch 11.
Row 1 (RS): 1 sc in 2nd ch from hook, (2 sc in next st, 1 sc in next st) 4 times, 2 sc in next st, turn. (15 sts)
Row 2: ch 1 (not counted as a st), 1 sc in each st to end, turn. (15 sts)
Row 3: 2 sc in next st, 1 sc in next 13 sts, 2 sc in next st, turn. (17 sts)
Row 4: ch 1, 1 sc in each st to end, turn. (17 sts)
Row 5: 2 sc in next st, 1 sc in next 15 sts, 2 sc in next st, turn. (19 sts)
Rows 6–9: ch 1, 1 sc in each st to end, turn. (14 Rnds of 19 sts)

NOTE: Do not fasten off and do not turn after Row 9. Next, work on the jacket's edge.

2 sc in last st of Row 9.

Work around the edge with 1 sc in each Row edge until you reach Row 4, 1 hdc in the edge of Row 4, 2 hdc in the

edge of Row 3, 2 hdc in the edge of Row 2, 1 sc in each st across the top of the jacket, 2 hdc in the edge of Row 2, 2 hdc in the edge of Row 3, 1 hdc in the edge of Row 4, 1 sc in the edge of each remaining row. Fasten off, leaving a long tail for attaching to the body. Turn the collar of the jacket out.

DOILY BASE
Using col 3, make a magic ring.
Rnd 1: ch 1, 10 sc in magic ring, join with ss. (10 sts)
Rnd 2: ch 1, 2 sc in each st around, ss to first sc. (20 sts)
Rnd 3: ch 1, (1 sc in next st, 2 sc in next st) 10 times, ss to first ch. (30 sts)
Rnd 4: ch 1, (1 sc in next 2 sts, 2 sc in next st) 10 times, ss to first ch. (40 sts)
Rnd 5: ch 1, (1 sc in next 3 sts, 2 sc in next st) 10 times, ss to first ch. (50 sts)
Next, make a scalloped edge around the base.
Rnd 6: ch 1, (1 sc in next st, (1 hdc, 1 dc) in next st, (1 dc, 1 hdc) in next st, 1 sc in next st, ss in next st) 10 times, ss to first ch. (70 sts)
Fasten off, leaving a long tail for attaching.

FINISHING

Have the following pieces ready before starting the finishing directions:
Head (x2), hair cap (x2), bride's hair style (if separate from head), groom's arms (x2), bride's arms (x2), groom's body, suit jacket, bride's body/dress, bouquet, groom's bow.

Using embroidery thread and a needle, sew a mouth onto each doll's face. Add eyelashes to the bride.

Place one hair cap onto the groom's head and sew it on. Sew bangs and hair details for the groom.

If using the bun style, stuff the bride's hair bun lightly. Place her hair bun over the remaining hair cap and sew it on. Then, place her hair cap over her head and sew it on.

Carefully place the groom's suit jacket around his body and sew it on. Sew the groom's arms onto his body. Take the bow and attach it onto his shirt by sewing or using a hot glue gun.

Sew the bride's arms onto her body.

Sew both heads onto the bodies.

Sew the bride's bouquet onto her arms and body, for extra stability.

Place both dolls on top of the doily base, and sew the bottoms of their bodies onto the doily base.

Note: For cake toppers, add a layer of protection between the doily and the cake. First, cut a plastic, laminated sheet of the same shape and size as the doily base. Then, use hot glue to secure the doily base onto the sheet. The doily base can then be placed on the cake without the yarn touching the icing.

Chubby Santa & elf

This chubby Santa and his elf helper are simple to make
as cute decorations for Christmas.

NAME: **LUCY COLLIN**
BIO: Lucy has been designing amigurumi for 7 years. Her children encouraged her to use her crochet skills to make them cute toys, and she then started to sell the patterns online. She has had two books published, including *Star Wars Crochet,* and has had several patterns included in various magazines. lucyravenscar.blogspot.com

DIFFICULTY:
★ ★ ☆ ☆ ☆

HOOK
E/4 (3.5mm)

YARN
In this project, we have used Stylecraft Special DK. You will need a DK weight yarn in your chosen colors.

Santa:
Color 1: Red (1 ball)
Color 2: White fuzzy yarn (1 ball)
Color 3: White (1 ball)
Color 4: Skin (1 ball)
Color 5: Black (1 ball)

Elf:
Color 1: Green (1 ball)
Color 2: Green (amount is included in col 1)
Color 3: Brown (1 ball)
Color 4: Skin (1 ball)
Color 5: Black (1 ball)
Color 6: Red (1 ball)

NOTIONS
Fiberfill
2 pairs 9mm safety eyes
Small bell for elf's hat
Yarn needle

MEASUREMENTS
3 ½" (8.9cm) tall

APPROX TIME TAKEN
2 hours

SPECIAL STITCH USED
Spike stitch (see page 158)

CHUBBY SANTA

HAT
Using the hook and col 1, ch 2.
Rnd 1: 6 sc into second ch from hook. (6 sts)
Rnd 2: (2 sc in next st, 1 sc in next st) 3 times. (9 sts)
Rnd 3: (2 sc in next st, 1 sc in next 2 sts) 3 times. (12 sts)
Rnd 4: (2 sc in next st, 1 sc in next 3 sts) 3 times. (15 sts)
Rnd 5: (2 sc in next st, 1 sc in next 4 sts) 3 times. (18 sts)
Rnd 6: (2 sc in next st, 1 sc in next 5 sts) 3 times. (21 sts)
Rnd 7: (2 sc in next st, 1 sc in next 6 sts) 3 times. (24 sts)
Rnd 8: (2 sc in next st, 1 sc in next 7 sts) 3 times. (27 sts)
Rnd 9: (2 sc in next st, 1 sc in next 8 sts) 3 times. (30 sts)
Rnd 10: (2 sc in next st, 1 sc in next 9 sts) 3 times. (33 sts)
Rnd 11: (2 sc in next st, 1 sc in next 10 sts) 3 times. (36 sts)
Rnd 12: 1 sc in each st around. (36 sts)
Rnd 13: (2 sc in next st, 1 sc in next 11 sts) 3 times. (39 sts)
Rnd 14: 1 sc in each st around. (39 sts)
Rnd 15: (2 sc in next st, 1 sc in next 12 sts) 3 times. (42 sts)
Rnd 16 (flo): 1 sc in each st around. (42 sts)
Change to col 2.
Rnd 17: 1 sc in each st around. (42 sts)
ss in next st, fasten off and weave in ends.

HEAD AND BODY
Note: The head is worked continuously from Rnd 16 of the hat, into the back loops only (blo) that remain after you have already worked into the front loops.

Holding the hat pointing downward, make a slip knot onto the hook using col 3 and join with a ss into the first back loop of Rnd 15.
Rnd 1 (blo): ch 1 (not counted as a st), 1 sc in same st at base of ch 1, 1 sc in each st around. (42 sts)
Rnd 2: 1 sc in each st around. (42 sts)
Rnd 3–5: 1 sc in next 14 sts, change to col 4, 1 sc in next 14 sts, change to col 3, 1 sc in next 14 sts**. (3 Rnds of 42 sts)
Rnd 6 (partial round): 1 sc in next 14 sts, (beard) 1 scflo in next 14 sts, ssflo in next st, ch 1, turn and work on these 15 sts only for beard.
Beard Row 1: Miss ss, 1 sc in next 12 sts, sc2tog, ch 1, turn. (13 sts)
Beard Row 2: Miss 1 st, 1 sc in next st, 1 hdc in next 2 sts, 1 dc in next 4 sts, 1 hdc in next 2 sts, 1 sc in next st, miss next st, ss in next st. (11 sts).
Fasten off and weave in ends.

Join in col 1 to the start of Rnd 6.
Rnd 7: 1 sc in next 14 sts, 1 scblo in next 15 sts (behind beard), 1 sc in next 13 sts. (42 sts)

Fix the eyes between Rnds 4 and 5, approximately 9 sts apart.

Rnd 8–10: 1 sc in each st around. (42 sts)
Change to col 5.
Rnd 11: 1 sc in each st around. (42 sts)
Change to col 1.
Rnd 12–13: 1 sc in each st around. (2 rnds of 42 sts)
Rnd 14: (sc2tog, 1 sc in next 5 sts) 6 times. (36 sts)
Rnd 15: (sc2tog, 1 sc in next 4 sts) 6 times. (30 sts)
Start to fill Santa with fiberfill.
Rnd 16: (sc2tog, 1 sc in next 3 sts) 6 times. (24 sts)

Rnd 17: (sc2tog, 1 sc in next 2 sts) 6 times. (18 sts)
Rnd 18: (sc2tog, 1 sc in next st) 6 times. (12 sts)
Rnd 19: (sc2tog) 6 times. (6 sts)
ss in next st, fasten off and weave in ends.

BOBBLE (FOR HAT)
Using col 2, ch 2.
Rnd 1: 6 sc into second ch from hook (6 sts)
Rnd 2: 1 sc in each st around. (6 sts)
ss in next st, fasten off, sew the hole shut, and sew the bobble to the top of the hat.

FINISHING

Using col 5, embroider a mouth. Finish stuffing Santa and close the hole neatly using a yarn needle.

CHUBBY ELF

Follow the instructions for Santa up to **, using the cols as given for the elf and working all rows of hat in col 1. Continue as follows:
Rnd 6: 1 sc in next 14 sts, change to col 4, 1 sc in next 14 sts, change to col 3, 1 sc in next 14 sts. (42 sts)
Change to col 6.
Rnd 7–8: 1 sc in each st around. (2 Rnds of 42 sts)

Fix the eyes between Rnds 4 and 5, approximately 9 sts apart.

Change to col 1.
Rnd 9: *1 sc in next st, spike stitch in next st; rep from * to end. (42 sts)
Rnd 10: 1 sc in each st around. (42 sts)
Change to col 5.
Rnd 11: 1 sc in each st around. (42 sts)
Change to col 1.
Rnds 12–19: Work as given for Santa pattern.

EARS (MAKE 2)
Using col 4, ch 2.
Rnd 1: 6 sc into second ch from hook. (6 sts)
Rnd 2: 2 sc in next 3 sts, (1 hdc, 1 dc) in next st, (1 dc, 1 hdc) in next st, ss in next st. Fasten off, leaving a length of yarn.

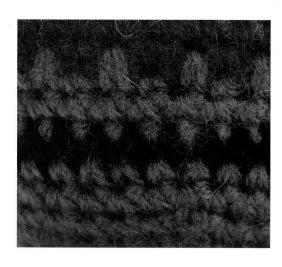

To make the ear more pointed, sew a stitch or two through the hdc and dc stitches, then thread the yarn through the ear to the opposite end to attach the ear to the head. Weave in any loose ends.

FINISHING

Sew a bell to the top of the hat using col 1.

Note: If you don't have a bell, you could make a bobble out of col 6 as follows:
Using col 6, ch 2.
Rnd 1: 6 sc into second ch from hook (6 sts)
Rnds 2–3: 1 sc in each st around. (2 Rnds of 6 sts)
ss in next st, fasten off, sew the hole shut, and sew the bobble to the top of the hat.

To turn them into Christmas tree decorations, take a length of ribbon, and use your crochet hook to pull it into the stitch behind the bobble or bell and through.

CHUBBY GNOME

To make Santa into a chubby gnome, simply work Rnd 17 of the hat in the same yarn as the rest of the hat and don't add a bobble. Work Rnds 7–10 of the body in any color you choose, then work rnds 12–19 in brown for the trousers of your gnome.

Reference

All the
information
you need
in one handy spot

Crochet glossary

amigurumi
The Japanese art of knitting or crocheting small, stuffed yarn creatures.

asterisk*
A symbol used to mark a point in a pattern row, usually at the beginning of a set of repeated instructions.

back loop (bl) only
A method of crocheting in which you work into only the back loop of a stitch instead of both loops.

back post (BP) stitches
Textured stitches worked from the back around the post of the stitch below.

ball band
The paper wrapper around a ball of yarn that contains information, such as fiber content, amount/length of yarn, weight, color, and dye lot.

block
A finishing technique that uses moisture to set stitches and shape pieces to their final measurements.

blocking wire
A long, straight wire used to hold the edges of crochet pieces straight during blocking, most often for lace.

bobble
A crochet stitch that stands out from the fabric, formed from several incomplete tall stitches joined at the top and bottom.

brackets [ ]
Symbols used to surround a set of grouped instructions, often used to indicate repeats.

chain (ch)
The most simple crochet stitch that often forms the foundation that other stitches are worked into.

chain space (ch-sp)
A gap formed beneath one or more chain stitches, usually worked into instead of into the individual chain(s).

chainless foundation
A stretchy foundation plus first row of stitches that are made in one step. Often used in flatwork pieces.

chainless foundation stitches
Stitches that have an extra chain at the bottom, so they can be worked into without first crocheting a foundation chain.

chart
A visual depiction of a crochet pattern that uses symbols to represent stitches.

cluster
A combination stitch formed from several incomplete tall stitches joined at the top.

contrast color (CC)
A yarn color used as an accent to the project's main color.

crochet hook
The tool used to form all crochet stitches.

crossed stitches
Two or more tall stitches that are crossed, one in front of the other, to create an X shape.

decrease (dec)
A shaping technique in which you reduce the number of stitches in your work.

double crochet (dc)
A basic stitch twice as tall as a single crochet.

drape
The way in which your crocheted fabric hangs; how stiff or flowing it feels.

draw up a loop
To pull up a loop of yarn through a stitch or space after inserting your hook into that stitch or space.

fan
A group of several tall stitches crocheted into the same base stitch and usually separated by chains to form a fan shape.

fasten off
To lock the final stitch with the yarn end so the crocheted work cannot unravel.

fasten on
To draw up a loop of new yarn through a stitch in preparation to begin crocheting.

foundation chain
A base chain into which most crochet is worked (unless worked in the round).

foundation stitches, chainless
See chainless foundation stitches.

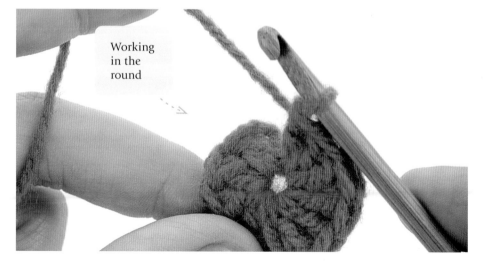

Working in the round

Top tip!
Use a yarn needle instead of a hook to weave the ends back through a project once complete. They will be more secure and less likely to unravel.

fringe
A decorative edging made from strands of yarn knotted along the edge.

frog
To unravel your crochet work by removing your hook and pulling the working yarn.

front loop (fl) only
A method in which you work into only the front loop of a stitch instead of both loops.

front post (FP) stitches
Textured stitches worked from the front around the post of the stitch below.

gauge (tension)
A measure of how many stitches and rows fit into a certain length of crocheted fabric, usually 4" (10.2cm), which indicates the size of each stitch.

half double crochet (hdc)
A basic stitch halfway between the height of a single and double crochet stitch.

increase (inc)
A shaping technique in which you add extra stitches to your work.

invisible finish
A method of finishing a round or edging so the join is not visible. This requires a yarn needle to finish.

knife grip
An overhand method of holding a crochet hook, similar to holding a knife.

linked stitch
A variation of any standard tall stitch that links the stitch to its neighbor partway up the post to eliminate the gaps between stitches and form a solid fabric.

loop stitch
A stitch that creates a loop instead of pulling the stitch through completely.

magic ring
A technique to begin working in the round without leaving a hole in the center by crocheting over an adjustable loop.

main color (MC)
The predominant yarn color of a project.

mattress stitch
A stitch to sew a seam that forms an almost invisible join on the right side of the work and a ridged seam on the wrong side.

motif
A crocheted shape usually worked in the round as a geometric shape and combined with other motifs into larger pieces.

parentheses ( )
Symbols used in crochet patterns to surround a set of grouped instructions, often used to indicate repeats.

pencil grip
An underhand method of holding a crochet hook, similar to holding a pencil.

picot
A tiny loop of chain stitches that sits on top of a stitch and creates a small shape.

popcorn
A combination stitch that stands out from the fabric formed from several tall stitches pulled together by a chain stitch.

post
The main vertical stem of a stitch.

post stitch
A stitch formed by crocheting around the post of the stitch in the row or round below, so the stitch sits in front of (or behind) the surface of the fabric.

puff stitch
A combination crochet stitch that forms a smooth, puffy shape created from several incomplete half double crochet stitches that are joined at the top and bottom.

repeat (rep)
To replicate a series of crochet instructions; one instance of the duplicated instructions.

Reference

reverse single crochet (rsc)
A variation of single crochet that is worked backward (left to right) around the edge of a piece, producing a corded edging.

right side (RS)
The side of a crocheted piece that's visible.

rip back
To unravel your crochet work.

round (rnd)
A line of stitches worked around a circular crocheted piece.

row
A line of stitches worked across a flat crocheted piece.

shell
A group of several tall stitches, crocheted into the same base stitch, that spread out at the top into a shell shape.

single crochet (sc)
The most basic crochet stitch.

skip (sk)
To pass over a stitch or stitches.

slip knot
A knot that can be tightened by pulling one end of the yarn; used for attaching the yarn to the hook to begin crocheting.

slip stitch (ss or sl st)
A stitch with no height, primarily used to join rounds and stitches to move the hook and yarn into a new position.

space (sp)
A gap formed between or beneath stitches, often seen in lace patterns.

spike stich
A stitch worked around existing stitches to extend down to one or more rows below, creating a long vertical spike.

stitch (st)
A group of one or more loops of yarn pulled through each other in a specific order until only one loop remains on the crochet hook.

stitch diagram
A map of a crochet or stitch pattern, where each stitch is represented by a symbol.

stitch marker
A small tool you can slide into a crochet stitch or between stitches to mark a position.

swatch
A crocheted sample of a stitch pattern large enough to measure the gauge and test the pattern with a specific hook and yarn.

tail
A short length of unworked yarn left at the start or end of a piece.

tension (gauge)
See gauge.

together (tog)
A shaping technique in which you work two or more stitches into one to reduce the number of stitches.

treble crochet (tr)
A basic stitch three times as tall as a single crochet stitch.

turning chain (t-ch)
A chain made at the start of a row to bring your hook and yarn up to the height of the next row.

V
The two loops at the top of each stitch that form a sideways V shape; standard crochet stitches are worked into both these loops.

V stitch
A group of two tall stitches crocheted into the same base stitch and separated by one or more chains, forming a V shape.

weave in
A method used to secure and hide the yarn tails by stitching them through your crocheted stitches.

whip stitch
A simple stitch to sew a seam by inserting the needle through the edge of both crocheted pieces at once to form each stitch.

working in the round
Crocheting in a circle instead of back and forward in straight rows, particularly used in amigurumi projects.

working loop
The single loop that remains on your hook after completing a crochet stitch.

wrong side (WS)
The side of a crocheted piece that will be hidden; the inside or back.

yardage
A length of yarn, usually expressed as an estimate of the amount of yarn required for a project.

yarn needle
A wide, blunt-tipped needle with an eye large enough for the yarn to pass through that's used for stitching crocheted pieces together and weaving in ends.

yarn over (yo)
To pass the yarn over the hook so the yarn is caught in the throat of the hook in order to create longer stitches.

yarn tail
See tail.

yarn weight
The thickness of the yarn (not the literal weight of a ball or yarn).

Abbreviations

US stitch name	Abbreviation	Description
back loop only	blo	The loop farthest from you at the top of the stitch.
back post single crochet	BPsc	Yarn over, insert the hook from the back to the front, then to the back around the post of the next stitch, yarn over and draw up a loop, (yarn over and draw through two loops) twice.
chain(s)	ch(s)	Yarn over and draw through the loop on the hook.
chain space(s)	ch-sp(s)	The space beneath one or more chains.
double crochet	dc	Yarn over, insert the hook into the next stitch and draw up a loop, (yarn over and draw through two loops on the hook) twice.
double crochet 2 together	dc2tog	(Yarn over, insert the hook into the next stitch and draw up a loop, yarn over and draw through two loops on the hook) twice, yarn over and draw through all three loops on the hook.
front loop only	flo	The loop closest to you at the top of the stitch.
front post double crochet	FPdc	Yarn over, insert the hook from the front to the back to the front around the post of the next stitch, yarn over and draw up a loop, (yarn over and draw through two loops) twice.
half double crochet	hdc	Yarn over, insert the hook into the next stitch, draw up a loop, yarn over and draw through all three loops on the hook.
repeat	rep	Replicate a series of given instructions.
single crochet	sc	Insert the hook into the next stitch and draw up a loop, yarn over and draw through both loops on the hook.
single crochet 2 together	sc2tog	(Insert the hook into the next stitch and draw up a loop) twice, yarn over and draw through all three loops on the hook.
skip	sk	Pass over a stitch or stitches—do not work into it.
slip stitch	ss (sl st)	Insert the hook into the next stitch, draw up a loop through the stitch and the loop on the hook.
stitch(es)	st(s)	A group of one or more loops of yarn pulled through each other in a specified order until only one remains on the crochet hook.
treble (triple) crochet	tr	Yarn over twice, insert the hook into the next stitch and draw up a loop, (yarn over and draw through two loops on the hook) three times.
turning chain	t-ch	The chain made at the start of a row to bring your hook and yarn up to the height of the next row.
yarn over	yo (yrh)	Pass the yarn over the hook so the yarn is caught in the throat of the hook.

Special stitches

Expand your stitch repertoire and apply some more advanced stitches to your amigurumi projects.

While most amigurumi is completed with the simple single crochet, some patterns require you to use more advanced techniques. Here we have included the special stitches that occur throughout this book, from the simple spike stitch to the slightly more difficult reverse single crochet. You will find some of these stitches appear several times, but they are all really easy to complete—true for most crochet stitches. They almost entirely use the same movements and yarn over actions that you are used to, but with a different combination of steps. Don't let the term "special" put you off—these just take you away from the standard slip, single, double, half double, and treble stitches that you will be familiar with in basic amigurumi.

Loop stitch

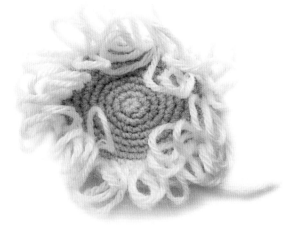

Spike stitch

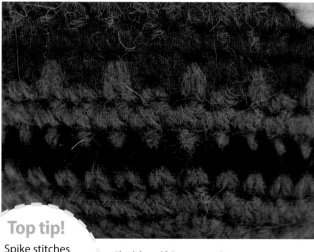

Top tip!

Spike stitches are also known as long stitches and dropped stitches.

Chubby elf (page 146)
Instead of working the sc into the top of the stitch of the previous round, work it into the stitch on the row below (from the round before). You can do various lengths of spike stitch by working in different rows.

Yeti/Bigfoot (page 92)
Insert the hook into the stitch, take the yarn under the hook then over your middle or forefinger to make a loop. Make the loop about 1" (2.5cm) long, but don't worry about making each one the same length. Pull the bottom of the loop (two strands) through. There are now 3 loops on the hook. You can pull the yarn to make the loop smaller if necessary, yo, then pull through all 3 loops.

Bobble stitch

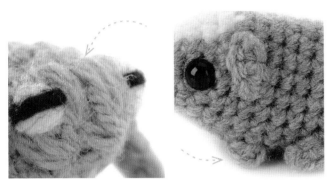

Frog (3sc-bob) (page 114)
yo, insert hook into next stitch, yo and pull back through stitch, yo, pull through first 2 loops, *yo, insert hook into same stitch, yo and pull back through stitch, yo, pull through first 2 loops; rep from * once more, yo, pull through all 4 loops on hook.

Baby guinea pigs (4dc-bob) (page 120)
yo, insert hook in stitch, yo and pull loop back through stitch, yo and pull through first 2 loops on hook; rep from * to * 3 more times always working into the same stitch, yo and pull through 5 loops on hook.

Popcorn stitch

Cup of bear (3dc-pop) (page 136) and **Yeti/Bigfoot** (6dc-pop) (page 92)
Work 3 or 6 dc into 1 st, work 3 or 6 dc into next st, remove hook from working loop, insert hook through both loops of first dc, and pull working loop through.

Cluster

Rob the raptor (page 72)
3 sc into the same st, then drop loop from hook. Reinsert hook into first sc of the 3 sc stitches you just made, then replace your dropped loop back over onto your hook and pull loop all the way through—1 cluster complete.

Reverse single crochet

Cup of bear (rsc) (page 136)
Also known as a crab stitch, this twists your stitches so that the usual V formation is hidden and the edge is neatly finished.

Yarn over (yo) and draw up a loop, making sure your hook faces toward the left as it would usually. If you twist your hook, you will end up with a mirrored version of a standard single crochet (sc), not a reverse stitch.

Now, complete the stitch as you would a normal single crochet, yarn over and draw through both loops on the hook. Continue to work backward along your edge, making sure that you don't accidently twist your hook!

Index